ROLLS-ROYCE
THE MERLIN AT WAR

By the same author

ROLLS-ROYCE: THE GROWTH OF A FIRM
ROLLS-ROYCE: THE YEARS OF ENDEAVOUR

Lord Hives, C.H.

ROLLS-ROYCE

THE MERLIN AT WAR

IAN LLOYD

First published 1978 by
THE MACMILLAN PRESS LTD
London and Basingstoke
Associated companies in Delhi
Dublin Hong Kong Johannesburg Lagos
Melbourne New York Singapore Tokyo

Printed in Great Britain at The Pitman Press, Bath

British Library Cataloguing in Publication Data

Lloyd, Ian
    Rolls-Royce, the Merlin at war.
    1. Rolls-Royce – History
    2. Airplanes, Military Motors – History
    3. Aircraft industry – & Great Britain
    I. Title
    338.7′62′3746   HD9711.G74R/

ISBN 0-333-24016-2

To the memory of
ERNEST HIVES
Mechanic
Companion of Honour
Doctor of Science
Peer of the Realm
Defender of Freedom

Contents

List of Illustrations

Preface

The history of Rolls-Royce during the Second World War is at once both more complicated and more straightforward than its history in the First World War, which I attempted to relate in *The Growth of a Firm*. Though many were lost or destroyed, some by enemy action, more records and documents had survived and most of the events had occurred within the memory of many post-war employees whom I was able to interview. It was difficult not to be swamped by the vast mass of memoranda, brochures and correspondence which the war generated and to select from this overwhelming volume of evidence those relevant facts which might, in all probability, have been lost to the historian of the future. His task would have been much more difficult if some attempt had not been made to correlate them with the evidence which already exists. This is still growing, though possibly at a declining rate, with the continual publication of journals, memoirs, official and unofficial histories about the war.

In writing the history of this period it was difficult to avoid two extreme points of view, from either of which the record would have appeared relatively coherent and consistent. The first of these would have confined the subject to the purely internal affairs of the company. The second would have related the history of the company to the general history of the war, in isolation from which the former could not really have been understood. Throughout the war Rolls-Royce policy was intimately and immediately related to the general trend of the war in the air in all theatres and to the overall industrial and armaments policy of the Government. An economic history written solely from the former point of view would have been unduly introspective, and, because of the dependence of internal policy on external policy and events, would provide a very incomplete record. A history written from the latter point of view, quite apart from the fact that it would have an undertaking of considerable magnitude requiring several volumes in its own right, would be a history of the war rather than a history of Rolls-Royce, and the firm could claim only a very small proportion of the attention which the intrinsic interest of its own history deserves.

What follows is inevitably a compromise which will probably suffer most of the defects of Cook's Tours of Normandy in 1946. In the earlier days of the war when the fate of England and the world depended quite literally on the efforts of the men at Derby, it is unfortunate that heads of departments were not encouraged to keep war diaries similar to those kept by ships of the fleet, squadrons of the R.A.F. and regiments of the line. There was naturally no time for this once the war had started, and in consequence there is no continuous and reliable record of what actually happened, of what decisions were taken and why they were taken. In peace as well as in war such a record would have been valuable, not only from the historical point of view. The minutes of important meetings have not always survived, and those which have were often scattered and incomplete. Important policy files had already been lost and in this respect the ravages of indifference are often more arbitrary than those of time. Nevertheless considerable material which, if not in itself historically complete, was of great interest and value, had survived; and this justified an attempt to construct a picture of these years which will at least provide a framework upon which something more thorough and complete can later be built.

I have entitled this volume *The Merlin at War*. Although the names of many other engines are mentioned in it, the Merlin was *the* key product of *the* key company in the British war effort. Without it the main fighter, bomber and reconnaissance squadrons of the R.A.F. would have lacked speed, height and endurance. Its continued development and production was therefore a matter of the utmost importance. The British people and the men of the R.A.F. were aware of this, not because they were necessarily in a position to make an appreciation of these factors, but because as the war progressed the skies of Britain were filled with a sound which gradually came to dominate the night as well as the day. The deep throb of the Merlin, unforgettable to those who heard it, was first generated by small groups of Hurricane and Spitfire fighters. By September 1940 the Squadrons were operating in wings and groups and, as the Battle of Britain was joined, it was not only the Air Staff and the pilots who came to realise that the performance of the R.A.F. depended not only on the courage of its pilots and the skill of its strategists and commanders, but on the power and reliability of the Merlin. As the war moved over from the defensive to the offensive, the Merlin powered into the air increasing numbers of Halifaxes, Lancasters, Mosquitoes, Mustangs and other aircraft. The thousand-bomber raids were put aloft by several thousand

Merlins. The skies of Britain and Europe reverberated to the deep throb of more than a million Merlin horse-power. This was the authentic voice of British air-power, a lion's roar which no cartoonists dared to disparage. The creation and sustenance of its principal component, the Merlin, is the central theme of this book.

November 1977 I.S.L.

Acknowledgements

The detailed acknowledgements made in the first volume of this history, *The Growth of a Firm*, cover most of the material in this book. I would like particularly, however, to acknowledge once again my debt to Professor M. M. Postan, then Professor of Economic History at Cambridge, for his wide-ranging assistance during the latter stages of my research on Second World War material. He not only made available to me, long before their official publication, several of the more relevant volumes of the *History of the Ministry of Aircraft Production*, but was instrumental in making arrangements for me to meet many of the key officials who were involved. H. H. Ellmere, at the Admiralty Record Office, J. C. Nerney and A. W. Savage at Air Ministry Records, Rear-Admiral M. S. Slattery, C.B., the Vice-Controller (Air) at the Admiralty, and many others who then had an intimate knowledge of these events showed a continuing interest in the attempt I was making to salvage some of the history of this period before it disappeared.

To the small group of enthusiasts at Rolls-Royce who took such immense pains to unearth long-forgotten documents and describe events which had often created no papers – Gordon Strangeways, Alan Swinden, W. A. Robotham, R. B. Wilson, Lord Hives himself and his indefatigable personal secretary, Miss Wilkinson – I owe a debt which this volume can never repay. They ensured that the early drafts were purged of some of their more elementary and glaring errors. Those which remain are entirely my responsibility.

Maurice Olley, at that time the cheerful and enthusiastic Chief Engineer of Vauxhall Motors, but always a Rolls-Royce man at heart, read and greatly improved the chapters dealing with Packard Merlin production in the U.S.A. The late P. W. S. Andrews, Fellow of Nuffield College, Oxford, contributed a virtual encyclopaedia of detailed and informative comment.

I am indebted to Sir Maxwell Aitken for permission to publish the photograph of Lord Beaverbrook on p. 36.

There is little doubt, as I suggested in the Preface to the first volume in this series, *The Growth of a Firm*, that some of the controversy which I describe in these pages was largely responsible for the long delay in the appearance of this history. Most of the individuals concerned were still alive. The arguments about policy had been conducted with passion and conviction on both sides. The fate of a nation and men's lives were indirectly at stake. Reputations, careers and much else besides had turned on the outcome. In some cases their experiences reinforced or, quite possibly, diminished strongly-held political beliefs about the nature of the political and economic organisation of the country which some hoped to develop when the war was over. All these events can now be viewed much more dispassionately. Calmer judgements can be made. Other crises have, in Rolls-Royce and in the national context, made even the traumatic events of the Second World War seem somewhat remote and unimportant.

Lord Hives, to whom this volume is dedicated, despite his decision to delay its publication for many years, died after a long and most tragic illness in 1965. It was he who wrote the simple, elegant and moving dedication at the foot of the beautiful stained-glass memorial window at the Nightingale Road headquarters of the company which is illustrated on page 141:

THIS WINDOW COMMEMORATES THE PILOTS OF THE ROYAL AIR FORCE
WHO, IN THE BATTLE OF BRITAIN, TURNED THE WORK OF OUR HANDS
INTO THE SALVATION OF OUR COUNTRY.

He was far too modest and unassuming a man, too busy 'working till it hurts', to have included his own hands amongst those which contributed to victory. Yet there is no doubt that the success of the Rolls-Royce war effort owed much to his imagination, determination and relentless energy. He was a great engineer, in the highest traditions of Sir Henry Royce, carrying considerable and expanding responsibilities in the years shortly before he became Chairman and Chief Executive. Yet he always found time to give encouragement and support to what must have been, for him, a most academic enterprise. No man more richly deserved the honours which he received. Though he called himself a 'mere mechanic', the Doctorate of Science awarded him by Cambridge University in 1951 was a much truer indication of his stature as a technologist. I greatly regret that he did not live to see the final publication of this book. But had he done so he would certainly have passed on all the credit to his colleagues.

1 Stalemate in Europe

The main expansion in the basic structure of the Rolls-Royce organisation – its physical capacity, administration and technical resources – had already taken place by the middle of 1939. The outbreak of war was not unexpected, as in 1914, and a great many contingency plans had been made. The works was not closed when the sirens blew and this time no employees were dismissed. The pace changed at once from top gear to overdrive. Chassis production, employing 2000 men, was immediately discontinued and the chassis shop was converted into the aero-engine repair section – a section which was to play a most critical part in the summer and autumn of 1940. The air-raid shelters which existed at the outbreak of war were sufficient for only 2500 of the 8000 employees, but by 25 September this had been increased by energetic measures to 5500. It was immediately decided to remove from the main Rolls-Royce engine works in Derby at Nightingale Road the maximum number of employees who were not engaged on direct production, and the necessary accommodation was discovered several miles outside Derby at the village of Belper. The entire drawing, technical and commercial staffs and all jig and tool designers, draughtsmen and tracers were transferred away from the works. Two shifts were set to work completing the camouflage of the factory, which was finished in two weeks. In the factory two shifts of ten hours per day were worked. Special classes were started in the instruction school to familiarise chassis division employees with the peculiarities of aero-engine production techniques. The main product of the company at this time, the Merlin, was in full production at Derby and Crewe, its technical and economic characteristics were thoroughly known, and though the problems of 1939 were no smaller in magnitude, they were completely different in type from those with which the management had to contend in 1914.

Though the aero-engine industry was to expand enormously in physical size as well as in the volume of resources which it employed, it did exist as an acknowledged industry in 1939, and the immediate directions in which it was to expand had been determined long before the outbreak of war. The government had expected a 'blitzkrieg', and the Air Council had calculated on the basis of front-line losses of 500 aircraft a month from a fully and continually engaged force of 1000 aircraft. The later expansion schemes of the rearmament period (Schemes F and L) had been designed to provide the reserves from which these losses could be replenished while the aircraft firms were getting into their stride. Many vicissitudes of this expansion were obviously not foreseen but the objectives were much clearer and more definite than in 1914. There was little doubt about the general character of the war which lay ahead. By far the most outstanding difference between the two periods, however, as reflected in the history of the company, is the almost exclusively physical and technical nature of the problems of management. Before the outbreak of war, costs and prices still exercised some constraint on the policies of the Air Ministry. After war had broken out the sole objectives of the Air Ministry, the Ministry of Aircraft Production, and the management of the company were to maximise output and performance.

There was room for a wide divergence of views as to how these objectives could most consistently and effectively be reached but there was an implicit assumption on both sides – which was not reached until a much later stage of the First World War – that the cost of production was important only in so far as it had to be controlled to avoid waste. Finance became quite simply a means to an end and financial policy consequently does not bulk very large in the history of this period. The management was naturally concerned to preserve the economic strength of the organisation and realised the importance of creating and maintaining reserves from which post-war reconversion could be financed. But the minor importance of this objective was kept in due proportion to all the others and it did not obtrude into the discussion. On the other side the vital importance of Rolls-Royce production to the war effort and the knowledge that this was very closely dependent on the capacity of the existing management – which there was no question of controlling or superseding – ensured that the attitude of the Ministries did not become unduly dominated by the general rules and regulations governing prices and profit margins. There was a complete unanimity of interest and outlook on everything that really mattered. It is all too easy to take this for granted and it is in fact a remarkable tribute to the breadth of mind and singleness of purpose of the responsible officials both at Derby and at the Ministries.

There was a clear realisation that anything which gave the appearance of conflict between the firm and the state was likely to be artificial – a product of misunderstanding which could always be resolved by referring it to the ultimate objective of winning the war. The really significant aspects of the history of this period are not financial, and only indirectly economic, in character. The economic problem became national in its scope. For each individual firm it was a question of making the best use of such resources as were placed at its disposal or, as often happened, it succeeded in placing at its own disposal. The accounts merely indicated their volume and disposition and provided information which was necessary for the control of production.

On 1 September 1939, the industry was operating under what was known as Scheme L, the expansion programme which had been adopted in April 1938 and which envisaged the production of 12,000 aircraft in two years. The succeeding plan, Scheme M, which was already under discussion, required the production of a further 12,000 aircraft and included the more modern type of fighters – the Whirlwind, Tornado and Typhoon – which had been designed round the Rolls-Royce Vulture and the Napier Sabre, and were expected to be the logical successors to the Hurricane and Spitfire. The heavy bombers included in this programme were the Manchester, the Halifax and the Stirling.

The Air Council had expected war to break out in October 1939 and had estimated that aircraft production would attain the figure of 2000 per month within eighteen months. Preparations to achieve this began in March 1939 for components and materials, but for airframes and engines existing capacity, enlarged by sub-contracting, was considered to be adequate. The Cabinet held the view that the war would last three years and the Secretary of State for Air, Sir Kingsley Wood, suggested that plans should be made to achieve an output of 3000 aircraft per month. After the supply of labour had been reviewed this figure was reduced to 2550 (including a small number from the Dominions). The senior Air Ministry official responsible for aero-engine production, Air Chief Marshal Sir Wilfrid Freeman, thought that this target would be reached in June 1942, and that output might ultimately be stepped up to 3000 by the end of June 1943. At this stage of the war manpower was considered to be the limiting factor. The target for home production was ultimately fixed at 2425 by July 1942, and this programme became known as the Harrogate programme. But

in the early stages of the war this programme had little or no effect on
Rolls-Royce. Orders were based on confirmed 'Instructions to Proceed'
(I.T.P.s) and the total of engines for which I.T.P.s had been received
was well below the total required by the various programmes now
being issued with ever-increasing frequency.

In September 1939 there were four main aero-engine firms –
Rolls-Royce, Armstrong-Siddeley, Bristols and Napiers; and six
shadow factories, excluding Crewe, which came under the direct
administration of the parent company, and Glasgow, which started the
production of parts in the middle of 1940 and produced its first
complete engine in November. All pre-war estimates of the capacity of
these factories were based on the assumption of single-shift working.
The main combat aircraft of the Royal Air Force were largely powered
by Bristol and Rolls-Royce engines, and the training and auxiliary
aircraft by Armstrong-Siddeley and De Havilland engines. Napiers had
produced no engines of any great importance after their 'Lion', though
the 'Sabre' was beginning to attract considerable attention at the Air
Ministry in 1939.

Between January and the end of August 1939 Derby had produced
1357 engines, the great majority of which were Merlins. A radial
air-cooled engine designed primarily for the new Fairey Fleet Air Arm
aircraft and known as the Boreas or Exe, was under development but

1. The Rolls-Royce V-12 cylinder Merlin Mark 61

not in production. The Peregrine (a supercharged Kestrel), the Vulture (a 24-cylinder X), and the Griffon (a Merlin scaled up to the same dimensions as the original 'R') were under development at Derby and work was in progress on a two-stroke engine and on compression ignition. Orders for these engines during 1939 had been based, albeit rather vaguely, on the 'L' scheme and in February Hives (General Manager and effectively the chief executive in charge of aero-engine production) informed Sir Wilfrid Freeman that the firm was 'planning to produce the equivalent of 600 Merlins per month in 12 months' time'. This estimate did not include the Glasgow factory, which was not scheduled to come into production until late in 1940, and it proved optimistic by two months. In the event there was no sudden rise in output towards the latter part of 1939 or early in 1940 and though there were many other reasons for this, which are discussed below, the fact that the absorption of engines into aircraft was substantially lower than output was responsible for a somewhat sceptical attitude towards the Air Ministry's demands that output should be further increased and capacity further expanded.

At the beginning of 1939 the confirmed orders for Derby were expected to produce an output of 3200 engines (almost entirely Merlins) by March 1940. Follow-on orders left a total of 4900 engines (400 of which were Vultures) to be completed after this and the company was warned that it might also be asked to produce no less than 1600 Peregrines for the Whirlwind. The Air Ministry was unable to give a clear indication of its future requirements until after the outbreak of war and all attempts during the early part of the year to obtain a delivery programme extending beyond March 1940 failed to produce any results.

During June and July 1939, however, the view that aircraft output would ultimately be limited by engine output began to crystallise at the Air Ministry. Despite the rapidly increasing gap between output and absorption in airframes, Air Marshal Tedder, as he was then, told W. Lappin, the firm's special representative at the Ministry, that he estimated there would be a shortage of 1000 Merlins by June 1940. The position was confusing to management since the requirements of the various programmes (of which no less than six were received in 1939 alone) varied greatly and were often apparently unrelated to the plans of the aircraft manufacturers, most of whom kept in direct touch with Derby.

As war became imminent, however, the question of contract cover

ceased to be of much significance since it became quite reasonable to
assume that this had become a mere formality. In August the 'all-out'
instructions began to come in from the Air Ministry. On the 26th Sir
Henry Self informed the managing director, Sir Arthur Sidgreaves that
it was 'of vital importance in the national interest that every practicable
step be taken immediately to intensify production of aircraft and
aeronautical material of all kinds required for the R.A.F. I am accordingly to request you to take immediate action by overtime working and
the institution of night shifts to accelerate at once and to the utmost
practicable extent the execution of the Air Ministry contracts on which
you are at present engaged.' He asked the firm to instruct all its
sub-contractors to do likewise.

On 28 August Sir Wilfrid Freeman wrote to Hives stressing the view
that engines would be the main factor limiting the supply of aircraft to
the R.A.F. 'I realise,' he said, 'that you have done a great deal towards
improving the position but if there are any further steps you can take to
improve output, and if there is any way in which I can help, or if you
have any suggestion to make towards a solution of the problems which
are outside your control, I hope you will not hesitate to inform me.'

This prompted an immediate reply in which Hives discussed the
various ways in which output from the Rolls-Royce group might be
increased. The very high Air Ministry (A.I.D.) inspection standards
resulted in a lot of scrapped materials which he thought could be
turned into perfectly satisfactory and reliable engines. Lead-bronze
bearings, for example, were scrapped if they were found to have
blow-holes, and these made no difference to their performance or
reliability. 'For years', he said, 'we have made a practice of running
engines built up with parts which have been scrapped by the A.I.D.,
and therefore we have that experience to draw upon.' The high quality
of screw-threads demanded on certain parts where it was not really
necessary restricted the output of sub-contractors who were not used to
high-precision work. External finish was costly and time-consuming
and did not affect the life or performance of the engine in the least. The
Royal Air Force would gain, he suggested, by relying much more fully
on Rolls-Royce engineers: 'The main point we wish to stress is that we
have the knowledge and experience and should be given the power to
say which parts should be used.'

In the same memorandum Hives made several further recommendations of great practical importance. He asked that Rolls-Royce should
be given the power to requisition all sub-contractors' plant and to

transfer this plant from one factory to another if this was considered to be necessary in the interests of maximum production. The next recommendation (which was immediately adopted and proved an outstanding success) was that a Rolls-Royce service engineer, who would report back directly to Derby, should be attached to every squadron flying aircraft fitted with Rolls-Royce engines. Even before official approval for this had been given a group of service engineers had left for France. The remaining recommendations concerned engines under development. Though Hives thought that the development of the Vulture, Boreas and Peregrine should be suspended, he was strongly in favour of continuing work on the Griffon, an engine whose overall dimensions and design were similar to the Merlin, which it could replace in several types of aircraft without serious modification to the airframe.

Sir Wilfrid Freeman agreed immediately to most of these suggestions. He was not altogether happy about suspending work on the Boreas, which was urgently required for Fairey naval aircraft, but Hives pointed out that the effort required to produce 275 Boreas engines was equivalent to 1200 Merlins and outlined a somewhat novel form of the conflict between firm and State.

> If we take the Rolls-Royce point of view it would be in our interests to proceed with the production of that engine. We have done three or four years work on it: – we are satisfied that as a type it has considerable merit over the radial sleeve-valve engine and we are definitely going to be the losers if the production of this engine is held up. From a national point of view, however, we think it would be wrong to proceed with this engine.

Freeman was persuaded and agreed to suspend work on the Boreas. Work on the Vulture had to continue, since it was assumed that the Manchester bomber and the Tornado fighter would use this engine. During the first few weeks of the war there was considerable uncertainty over the Peregrine. The order was first reduced, then increased, and finally cancelled. The Air Ministry was also unable to reach a clear decision about the Merlin-engined Wellington bomber. The Alvis Company had already started a power-plant production line to adapt Merlins to this aircraft, and after considerable discussion it was decided that the work should proceed. The Air Ministry wished to suspend the Merlin Wellington on the grounds that there would be a very great expansion of the output of other types of aircraft for which

2. The Rolls-Royce X-24 cylinder vulture

no alternative engine existed; but Rolls-Royce was under no illusions, and it was realised that it would be a complete waste of resources if these engines were not used.

In the first week of September the whole organisation at Derby and Crewe was keyed up for the onslaught. It was naturally expected that aero-engine firms would be one of the highest-priority targets of the Luftwaffe and despite the dislocation involved in the transfer of staff there was a record output of 74 Merlins (of which nine were produced at Crewe). But the onslaught did not materialise and the people of Britain realised that the German armed forces were to be otherwise occupied for some time. For most people there was a sensation of 'back to normal'. The war did not greatly upset the customary routines of existence and this attitude reduced the sense of urgency and the flexibility which this induces, until the full weight of the Reichswehr was thrown into the attack on France. Only then was it realised that half-measures and total war were incompatible.

Though the psychological conditions of the 'phoney war' inhibited an immediate nation-wide response, there were, fortunately, a good many responsible people in the Ministries and at Rolls-Royce who were not deceived by the slow tempo of the first few months. They realised that in due course the demands which the industry would be called upon to meet would tax its capacity to the utmost. The existing capacity, though quite capable of fulfilling current orders, was unlikely to be able to meet the demands of the global air war which the realists foresaw to be inevitable as soon as Hitler had conquered Europe. Though Hives was in full agreement with the Ministry's view that capacity would have to be increased he did not consider that equipping completely new factories was the best way to do it.

Before the war actually had broken out the Air Ministry had begun to urge the erection of a duplicate Glasgow factory with a similar planned capacity of 400 Merlins per month. There was no time to build a completely new factory and in the initial stages it was decided to request the Austin Company, which was already running an airframe Shadow Factory, to convert their Longbridge works to Merlin production. On 15 August Major Bulman, a senior Air Ministry official, wrote to Hives asking him to 'consider planning the Austin Motor Company's war potential for Merlin production as soon as you and Mr. Lord return from leave'. The Austin Company considered this to be a rather vague directive, but with the assistance of some planning engineers from Derby two alternative schemes were rapidly prepared. The first scheme was intended to give Rolls-Royce 'the maximum assistance at the minimum cost' by utilising wherever possible the existing machine tools and facilities at Longbridge, the main Austin car production works. This was in reality the equivalent of a considerable increase in sub-contract capacity, but the load on the three assembly factories (Derby, Crewe and Glasgow), of which only one was in full production, would have been greatly increased. The Air Ministry was not in favour of this and wanted complete Merlins produced and assembled at Longbridge. To do this Austins estimated that they would have to supplement the capacity of the Longbridge plant by a completely new works of 836,000 sq. ft. Only 1008 machine tools out of a total of 3226 were adaptable to Merlin production and they estimated that a further 1580 machine tools, costing over a million pounds, would be required. The capital cost of the entire scheme was estimated at £3 million with an additional £2–3 million for working capital. The Austin production engineers calculated that the interim period between the cessation of car production and the start of aero-engine deliveries would be 'at least twelve months'.

S. E. Blackstone, a very experienced production engineer who had advised the Rolls-Royce management in the planning and erection of Crewe and Glasgow, visited Longbridge on 19 September. He found that Austins were then planning to produce complete engines without any sub-contracting whatever, and that though many machines required adaptation their equipment was adequate for this purpose with the single exception of gear-grinding machine tools. The general scheme was to duplicate at Longbridge the carefully prepared layout of Glasgow.

This proposal was finally abandoned in favour of an alternative, but not before considerable preliminary work had been done at Longbridge. The Austin Company was heavily committed to the production of army transport of various kinds and after discussions with Sir Wilfrid Freeman it was decided that the entire proposition should be taken over by the Ford Company since its French subsidiary, Fordair, had been considering a proposal to manufacture Merlins in France for the French Government. This decision was reached in October and the Rolls-Royce officials, who were heavily overburdened as it was with the responsibility of Derby, Crewe and Glasgow, took no part in the discussions. The first intimation which Rolls-Royce received of the change in policy was the arrival of several Ford engineers at Derby, followed by a letter from Mr Lord, then managing director of Austins, informing Hives of the agreement which had been reached and offering assistance of limited sub-contract facilities wherever these were not required by the other commitments of the Austin Company.

A completely new works on the Glasgow scale was started at Trafford Park, Manchester, in February 1940 but though the Ford Company was naturally dependent on Rolls-Royce for a great deal of technical advice and assistance, the management of this works was in the hands of the Ford Company, and the details of its history do not come within the province of this study.

2 No Merlins for France

In 1939 the French aero-engine industry was unable to meet the demand for engines from its own airframe manufacturers; and in view of the world-wide reputation which the Merlin was rapidly acquiring for its performance in the Hurricane and Spitfire, the French Air Ministry decided to request Monsieur Dollfuss, managing director of the firm of Fordair, a subsidiary of the American Ford Company in France, to negotiate with Rolls-Royce for a licence to manufacture the Merlin. The original scheme was discussed in London in March 1939, and was not very ambitious. Monsieur Dollfuss pointed out confidentially to Colonel Darby, an experienced executive entrusted with the negotiations with the French Government, that his company was not really interested in making complete engines for some time. His intention was to work with Rolls-Royce 'on a basis of assembly'. During the course of discussions with Colonel Darby he put forward the view that the whole proposal had been made 'purely from the point of view of satisfying political opinion in France'.[1] In view of subsequent developments, these statements seem to have been particularly frank and prophetic. Though such remarks might have been expected to arouse the suspicions of the Rolls-Royce management that a great deal of drive would not be put into a production scheme designed purely to 'satisfy political opinion', this does not appear to have happened. The *bona fides* of the proposal were not questioned until the stampede of circumstances made it quite obvious that the French Government and its representatives in 1939 were quite incapable of formulating and executing a precise, definite and realistic policy.

But though the management would probably never have considered such a proposal had it been made after the outbreak of war, it must be remembered that in March 1939 an intelligent commercial policy had at least to cover the possibility that war would *not* break out. Under these circumstances an opportunity to increase the income to be obtained from the licence and subsequent manufacture of the company's products abroad could not be neglected. The entrepreneur does not usually base his commercial decisions on an interpretation of the

11

motives of his customer, but in large-scale enterprises, where possibility of loss cannot always be insured against by the normal commercial and legal safeguards, such interpretation becomes important. The opportunity cost[2] (if such it may be called) of the diversion of technical effort involved in the training of a completely new organisation in the production of a complex product like an aero-engine, though difficult to measure, is probably very great and easily outweighs, in the initial stages, the financial remuneration which such a licence brings in. This cost is of course much higher when the parent company is expanding its own organisation, as was the case with Rolls-Royce at this time.

The British Air Ministry, which was kept informed of the trend of these discussions throughout, agreed to the sale of manufacturing rights on certain conditions. The first of these was that the early Mark III Merlins could be released in connection with the contract and the building up of production in France, but not the later Merlin Xs. It was realised that there was no hope of the Fordair factory producing complete Merlins for the French aircraft manufacturers much before the spring of 1940, and in consequence in the initial stages the Amiot and Dewoitine French aircraft factories were to be dependent almost completely on Derby. At this stage the Fordair project was regarded by the French more as a scheme for providing repair, overhaul and test facilities for Merlins supplied from Derby. The project was regarded at Derby as a purely commercial transaction, and the prices quoted were commercial prices.[3] The manufacturing licence was sold directly to the French Government for £50,000 and on top of this there was a royalty of £200 per engine which would be proportionately reduced by the value of British-made parts in any complete engines assembled in France in the early stages. Similar conditions governed the production of spare parts. A clause in the contract which later gave rise to considerable misunderstanding entitled the French Government to negotiate a licence on similar terms for any future engines which Rolls-Royce might develop. The licence was sub-licensed to Fordair, the firm chosen to undertake the project.

The British Air Ministry laid down two further conditions. The first of these required Rolls-Royce to 'provide reciprocal information as regards design, maintenance, installation and other technical experience between yourselves and your licensee'. Any information received in this way was to be made available to the Air Ministry. The second condition was that Rolls-Royce would pay to the Air Ministry a proportion of the royalty payments. Both these conditions were agreed to by Rolls-Royce.

Before the final details of the agreement had been completed a number of Ford engineers arrived at Derby to gain a general idea of the manufacturing techniques involved in Merlin production. Some of these men were from the parent company in Detroit and had worked on the Liberty project in the First World War. These engineers were given full run of the Derby factory and spent about six months at Derby. Most of the information was passed back to Detroit, where the parent company was carrying out the production planning of the entire scheme. The special machine tools, none of which were obtainable in France, were all ordered and progressed from the Dearborn head-quarters of the Ford Company in Detroit.

Production was planned to start at the Ford Strasbourg plant while a new factory at Bordeaux was being completed. The original scheme envisaged the production of parts in four stages. The first were to be manufactured immediately, the second and third were to be brought into production as the scheme developed, and the fourth were to be manufactured at Derby. Output was expected to reach a figure of fifteen engines per week at the Bordeaux factory.

Fordair's contact with Derby was thus of a very indirect nature and, though Rolls-Royce more than fulfilled the letter and spirit of the contract in the supply of blueprints and technical knowledge, very little progress was made in the few remaining months before the outbreak of war. Fords at Detroit had at one stage considered using the tools of the Lincoln automobile plant for Merlin production, but this was quickly abandoned when some of the Rolls-Royce engineers who saw it pointed out its general unsuitability. In other respects, however, the planning work done at Detroit was very thorough – although Fords, through pressure on their own facilities, sub-contracted most of the work.[4]

The project did not fare so well in its execution in France. As early as July it appeared most unlikely that the French factories would be able to build up anything approaching an assembly line from their own parts. There was a severe shortage of jigs and tools (which were in short supply everywhere as a result of rearmament) and of specialised draughtsmen. In consequence it was decided that Rolls-Royce could best assist the project by supplying sets of almost complete engines which would be assembled in France. On 24 July Sir Wilfrid Freeman agreed to recommend to the Air Council a programme for the delivery of 75 sets of Merlin parts between September 1939 and January 1940. This was to be followed by a further 100 sets up until May 1940, and a further 50 between the end of May and August. It was expected that deliveries would begin early in 1940 and it was stipulated in the agreement that 125 of the first 250 engines would be returned to the Air Ministry. The Air Ministry was not prepared to forgo more than 125 engines at this stage, but the figure of 250 was agreed to help the French factory to achieve more continuous production.

On 21 August there was a completely unexpected development at Dearborn. Henry Ford, who was not impressed by Britain's or France's chances of defeating a sustained German attack, decided to keep his American plants strictly neutral. As a result of this decision all Merlin and other armament work of any description was rapidly cleared out of the Ford factories and organisation at Detroit. Work on the special machine tools for the Bordeaux factory was suspended, and though the orders for machine tools were not actually cancelled their makers were left uncertain as to their ultimate fate. All the American engineers in France were recalled to the United States. The situation was further complicated by the uncertainties and intricacies of the Neutrality Act.

The effect of all this on the French project was shattering. It soon became apparent that the French organisation and management had relied very heavily on the Detroit firm.[5] To complicate matters even further the French Government ordered the removal of the entire Strasbourg staff and movable plant to Bordeaux. The Bordeaux factory had been very fully equipped with standard machine tools and was almost ready to start production but most of the staff at Bordeaux were called up on the outbreak of war. The chaotic state of the administration, the remaining members of which were working sixty hours a week in an endeavour to get the factory running, the virtual cancellation of the special machines on order in the United States, and the fact, discovered by Rolls-Royce just before the outbreak of war, that the French factory intended to rely completely on the United States for supplies of raw materials, together presented a depressing picture.

A conference on the subject was called in London on 12 September at which M. Dollfuss, M. Ricardo of the French Air Ministry, and M. Panier of Fords were present. At this meeting Dollfuss explained what had happened in France and suggested that the French factory should now act as sub-contractors to Derby. For them to be able to do this, however, Rolls-Royce would have to provide the essential machine tools[6] and it was equally obvious that technical assistance would also have to be provided on a much greater scale than that contemplated in the original agreement. If Rolls-Royce was unable to provide this assistance, Dollfuss pointed out, the French factory would have to be employed in the manufacture of Hispano-Suiza engines. Hives did not intend to be saddled with the additional burden of getting the French factory into production. He suggested that Rolls-Royce would provide whatever assistance was within their power but that they could not be expected to tool up the French factory. He saw no reason why the tools should not still be obtained from the United States. The question of quantities was raised and Dollfuss pointed out that the French Government had, since the outbreak of war, doubled its original order for 1250 Merlins plus 30 per cent spares. This meant that the Bordeaux factory was required to plan for a production of twelve engines per day. It was generally agreed at the meeting that the idea of producing complete engines was somewhat too ambitious in view of the complications which had developed and that the best plan was for Derby to continue with the scheme to provide the French factory with sets of parts in an endeavour to build up production by stages. The idea was that the French factory would both supply parts and the complete engines assembled from the parts supplied from Derby and from Fordair direct to England. The complete engines would be tested at Derby and supplied to the French Government direct.

On 21 September Colonel Darby left for France to survey the whole organisation and report on the progress which had been made. Rolls-Royce had agreed to offer all possible help within reason on the condition that the French management took the main burden of responsibility for getting production started. A peculiar feature of the situation was the lack of liaison between the French and the English Ford Company at Dagenham. The latter had been asking the Air Ministry for work and Rolls-Royce could not understand why the French company did not seek their help. Before he left for France Colonel Darby contacted the Dagenham factory, discovered that they had tool capacity available, and cabled this information to Dollfuss.

Hives was very sceptical about the whole project and on 25 September he expressed serious doubts to Sir Wilfrid Freeman.

> My own views are that the French Company are just playing with the job; in fact I even doubt their honesty of purpose. The impression I have is that they have been given huge orders by the French Air Ministry for Ford trucks and they certainly have not the capacity to

tackle the Merlin job unless it operates as an entirely separate division. The promises which the French Ford Company made to the French Air Ministry to produce Merlin engines and parts were just ridiculous. It either meant they were thoroughly dishonest or that they had not grasped in any way the magnitude of the job they had undertaken.

A further meeting with the directors of the French company and representatives of the French Air Ministry was held at Duffield on 6 October. Hives was critical of the way in which the entire project was being handled and alleged that the French company had made no serious effort to get into production. He was opposed to the suggestion that the French company should manufacture so-called 'bottleneck' items, since the labels on the bottles were constantly varying and this did not provide a firm basis for an intelligent production plan. He was of the opinion that the French factory should still aim at the production of complete engines. If they planned to produce engines as soon as possible there was a possibility that they would at least produce parts. The American machine tools had been released by this time, which made this quite a feasible proposition and one which set the French management a clear and unequivocal target.

   A major objection raised by Monsieur Dollfuss to this proposal was that the capital of the French company (£1,600,000) was not large enough to finance the production of complete engines. He also complained that Rolls-Royce were not giving the French organisation the technical assistance which they had expected and which he considered to be implied in the contract. These recriminations were not helpful and the conference achieved very little. Hives was very dissatisfied and in a report to the board he reverted to the point of view that the most that could be expected of the French factory was assistance in the assembly of a small number of engines and in the production of selected parts for which they had the equipment.

   The accusation that Rolls-Royce have not been helpful is entirely untrue; in fact I will go so far as to say that our enthusiasm to help may have lulled Fordair into thinking that there was very little for them to do. . . . There have been endless discussions as regards the position of the plant and machinery in France, but the fact which stands out is that although these negotiations started last March, today there is not a single machine available in France ready to produce Merlin pieces. . . . Technical information is not a commodity which you can wrap up in a parcel and deliver, it can only be of value when it is conveyed to a person who understands and desires the knowledge. . . . Fordair have not grasped this fundamental point.

On 6 November H. J. Swift left for France and spent a week at the Fordair factory. His report, which was not entirely unfavourable and did not underrate the great efforts which had been made by some of the Fordair engineers, supported Hives's view that there was no clear objective and that the French management had greatly underestimated the complexity of aero-engine production.

Two factories were in operation at Bordeaux. The new plant was not ready to start production when the move from Strasbourg took place and in consequence a small plant at Poissy, just nearby, had been started on the production of tools. This factory, which was well designed and intended to employ 6000 men in a factory of 480,000 sq. ft., was only 60 per cent complete and employing only 600 men. There were no Fellowes gear-cutting machines and Swift did not expect the factory to produce a complete engine until September 1940 at the earliest. 'It seems obvious,' he wrote, 'from the nebulous state in both factories and from the machine tools and the small amount of skilled labour available that it is not likely that there will be any extensive production of components from France for a very long time to come.' A most serious problem was the 'crippling lack of skilled designers and toolmakers', and Swift concluded that until the American effort began to materialise very little could be expected from the factory.

The Rolls-Royce representative at Bordeaux confirmed Swift's opinion that it would be a long time before the factory turned out a complete Merlin, though he attributed this to the mass-production mentality.

> I am favourably impressed with the ability of the men I have met here. Their chief difficulty will be the enlistment of skilled men to assist them in the great effort they have undertaken. . . . They only think along the lines of Ford mass-production and in consequence they will not start producing till every gauge, tool and cotter pin is ready and at hand. . . . I am afraid it will be some time before a complete unit is off test and ready for delivery.

Willis was very critical of the poor managerial organisation. There was little positive control and no one would take responsibility. The course of these negotiations throws a very revealing light on the general state of the French aircraft industry in 1939. The position at the aircraft firms, which several Rolls-Royce representatives visited in the course of supervising the installation of Merlins in various production and prototype aircraft, was little better. By comparison, the picture in England was one of superlative organisation and efficiency.

The project was not heartily backed by the French Air Ministry, which always gave the impression of wanting to obtain something for nothing and adopted an indignant attitude when it was pointed out that the results would depend very largely on their own efforts. It is apparent that there was a great deal of politics involved on the French side and that the final cancellation of the manufacturing project on 18 December was the result of high-level intrigue in French military, political and commercial circles. The French, in 1940, clearly preferred politics to production.

On 9 December Monsieur Dollfuss wrote to Sidgreaves informing him that Rolls-Royce had not, in their opinion, fulfilled their obligations under the agreement: 'As I led you to anticipate at our last conference in Derby, the assistance which you were able to give us as regards assembly, tests and supplies of finished parts was judged inadequate by the French Air Ministry to ensure, together with our production, a sufficient output of Merlin X motors.' He informed Sidgreaves that the French Air Ministry intended to fulfil the other clauses of the contract and that in return for 'insisting on' clause 8 Rolls-Royce would be expected to fulfil all other orders. The letter concluded with a peremptory demand that Rolls-Royce should make available to the French Air Ministry the plans of all engines then under development. The licence had in fact contained an option, exercisable within five years, to produce new engines which Rolls-Royce put into production at Derby, the terms and conditions of production being subject to negotiation. Dollfuss's letter, which did not reach England until 28 December, ten days after the cancellation of the licence but clearly anticipating it, was an ineffective *tour de force* and an attempt to cover up the fact that the French had decided to produce the Hispano-Suiza engine at Bordeaux because the Merlin had proved beyond the capacity of the Fordair organisation.

Rolls-Royce did not in the least regret the loss of this commitment, which had absorbed an excessive amount of the valuable time of the company's senior officials and had achieved nothing. In a letter informing Maurice Olley of what had happened Hives said that he considered it to be 'the best thing that could have happened both as regards providing the maximum war effort and also to relieve us of one of our worries'. Even the payment of the quite clear-cut financial obligations of the French Government under the licence involved tedious negotiation and delay.

Though the project for manufacturing Merlins in France was completely abandoned, the French Air Force still required Merlin engines for two types of aircraft – the Amiot bomber and Dewoitine fighter – which it was intended should use them. By 11 April 126 engines had actually been delivered under the agreement between the British and French Air Ministries, and it appeared that the French intended to ask for another 200 engines when the 300 originally ordered had been delivered. By the fall of France, 143 Merlins had been delivered in all. This figure was substantially below that which the French Government had hoped for, but in view of subsequent events, and the fact that the aircraft firms seemed incapable of putting their aircraft into the air, it was in France's own interests that the remaining Merlins should remain in England to reinforce the strength of the R.A.F. From many points of view it is just as well that the resources of the Rolls-Royce management were not diverted, as they might easily have been, into building up a substantial and reliable unit for Merlin manufacture in France. This could only have been done at the expense of Derby, Crewe and Glasgow, and had it been successful the Germans would have been presented with a first-class organisation which they would not have hesitated to use. Nor could it be argued, in view of the facts presented above, that had the scheme matured more rapidly, this would have greatly increased the strength of the French Air Force. Such an achievement would have required a great deal more than the successful reorganisation of one factory.

3 The Packard Merlin

As soon as war broke out Hives raised the question of production in the United States. In a letter to Sir Wilfrid Freeman he advocated the production of selected parts which were likely to prove difficult items in England and for which the creation of additional capacity would have been either impossible or excessively costly in England. He considered that a carefully constructed programme of this type would achieve, for a given expenditure of dollars, a far greater increase in production than that which the import of an equivalent value of machine tools would make possible. There were two other factors of considerable importance. The Ford Company at Detroit had already received, and had been working on, a complete set of Merlin drawings on behalf of their subsidiary in France and had placed large orders for machine tools. It thus seemed logical that if any company should produce the Merlin in the United States it should be the Ford Company, but for various reasons which will be discussed later, this did not take place. The second point which Hives rightly stressed was that most of the machine tool equipment for the production of the difficult pieces of the Merlin was already obtained from the United States. A large amount of equipment had been ordered for Crewe and Glasgow and he suggested that it might be wiser to leave this in the United States where there was an abundance of skilled labour and little risk of enemy action. This argument was strongly supported by the fact that soon after the outbreak of war two ships carrying machine-tools for Rolls-Royce, the S.S. *Malabar* and the S.S. *City of Flint*, were torpedoed and sunk. But the optimum utilisation of British-owned resources in the United States was clearly a matter of high-level state policy and many of the problems involved had hardly been discussed at this stage. Hives concluded by stressing the need for speed. 'In the last war it took us two years before we appreciated the possibility of producing aero-engines in the United States. This time, if we mean business, whatever we can possibly do out there should be done as quickly as possible.'

The Government, unfortunately, did not share his sense of the opportune. At this early stage of the war the American Merlin project was too ambitious a proposal and Sir Wilfrid Freeman replied that although he liked it very much the country could not afford it. Hives did not agree with this and he argued that, within the limitations imposed by the general financial controls of the war economy, the firm would have to act independently to secure sources of supply in America. He immediately contacted Maurice Olley[1] at General Motors and succeeded in persuading him to act as the company's representative in America during the war. General Motors generously agreed to release him for the duration. Within a few weeks a subsidiary company, Rolls-Royce (Michigan), had been floated to handle the procurement of machine tools, parts and raw materials, largely on the initiative of J. McManus, the company's zealous legal representative in New York who had previously been secretary of the Springfield company.

The project for manufacturing Merlins in France had also made progress and all these factors, combined with the continually increasing stock of unabsorbed Merlins, caused the management at Derby to view with considerable scepticism any project which involved the erection of a completely new factory. Blueprints did not make Merlins and there was a limit to the amount of 'parenting' work which the Derby engineers could undertake without incurring the risk that development and production at Derby itself would suffer. A long war lay ahead and the human resources of the organisation were certain to be heavily overtaxed. At such times the expanding volume of important and interdependent decisions requiring the exercise of skilled judgement imposes a great strain on senior executives. New routines have to be created by trial and error. Many of the problems are completely novel, particularly when an industry is expanding on to a completely new level of production. Those who understand the product are unfamiliar with quantity production and those who understand quantity production are unfamiliar with the product and the limitations which its peculiarities impose on their techniques.[2] Both manufacturing techniques and products had to endure a process of mutual adaptation, the direction of the give-and-take varying greatly from component to component.

On 2 November, therefore, Hives wrote to Sir Wilfrid Freeman pointing out some of the discrepancies which he believed to have developed in the higher policy of the Air Ministry.

The 1941 Air Ministry engine programme calls for far less monthly output than the last six months in 1940. The present programme we are working to is considerably below the programme which was submitted to us in March of this year, and it was on the March programme that the Ford factory was planned. Our estimates show that by the end of 1941 we shall have produced 2,000 more Merlin engines than the latest Air Ministry programme and that by September 1942 we shall be 5,000 over the programme. . . . We are finding that with a standardised product like the Merlin we are exceeding our estimates for output. . . . We cannot see how the Ford factory which is to duplicate Glasgow fits into the Rolls-Royce aero production programme.

These were optimistic estimates which were not of course fulfilled, but they seemed reasonable enough at the time and indicate one of the important psychological properties of the 'programme' method of industrial control. The programme was an imperfect measure of controlling industrial output, and as the war progressed much was discovered about the relationship between programmes and output. From the outset Hives was somewhat sceptical of the purpose and efficacy of the 'programme'. The Air Ministry soon realised that it would have to bring in expert assistance from outside if these were going to be of any significance and endeavoured to persuade R. H. Coverley, then in charge of the Rotol factory, to join the Ministry as Director of Engine Production. Hives opposed this and told Freeman that Coverley would be wasted at M.A.P. 'It is difficult for us to understand', he said, 'what the duties of a D.E.P. entail. If we go by our experience the only discussions we have are on engine programmes which do not mean anything because they are altered every few weeks. We have given up worrying about the programmes, and have accepted that our problem is to produce as many engines as possible and to watch the aircraft constructors' output to see that we are making the right type of engine.' Freeman would not agree to Coverley staying at Rotols. 'I can assure you', he replied, 'that it is a full-time job for the D.E.P. since we are certainly going to run short of engines towards the end of the year. I do not think I am giving away any secret when I say that the cumulative deficiency of Bristol engines by the end of 1941 will exceed 2,500, and there is obviously no prospect of your firm being able to make good this deficiency.'

It was thus assumed at this stage that a more elaborate technique of programming would, almost of itself, ensure the increase in output.

The idea of the engine firms planning their own programmes on the basis of the aircraft constructors' requirements savoured too much of the chaotic price system. Once the system was fully developed the programme did enable a fairly high degree of co-ordination to be achieved but its most effective function was that of an instrument of measurement, *ex post facto*, rather than an instrument of control. At this stage, however, the information at the disposal of the Air Ministry was meagre and the techniques of programming and all the concomitant apparatus required to direct and co-ordinate the activities of what rapidly became the largest industry in the country had hardly begun to be developed. Even when fully developed they were more effective as a method of informing the planners than they were as a method of directing the activities of the firms.

On 12 December Hives informed Sir Wilfrid Freeman that Rolls-Royce was 'making considerable progress in our plans to find additional outlets for the surplus Rolls-Royce aero-engines'. The cumulative output at the end of January 1940 exceeded airframe demand by 1618 engines, and it was not until March that monthly absorption actually exceeded output. Total absorption exceeded output on only one other occasion (February 1941) but the real significance of the total figures is small and must be judged in relation to the figures for individual types of engines required for the production lines of specific types of aircraft.[3] The latest type of Merlin, especially in the later years of the war, was nearly always in short supply whereas there was nearly always a surplus of the oldest mark of engine still in production. Hives, having foreseen this development, made great efforts to retain the flexibility of the Derby factory, even at the expense of output.

During the first three months of 1940 there was a noticeable decline in the output both of new and repaired engines.[4] This state of affairs obtained throughout the industry. The total output of aircraft in February (719) was less than in September 1939 (781) and the output for March 1940 was not only below the wartime forecast but was also below the figure planned under the peacetime programme. This state of affairs was mainly the result of three factors, some of which applied as much to Derby as to the industry as a whole. Most influential of all was the general air of lethargy which had developed as a result of the failure of the blitzkrieg to materialise. The second was the fact that the managements of most concerns were too preoccupied with the problems involved in organising sub-contract programmes, in training sub-contract personnel in their new tasks, and in dealing with all the other irritations and delays caused by the wartime regime, to devote their attention to the problem of increasing the immediate output of their own plants.

The failure of output to rise was, paradoxically, an indication of the amount of energy and resources which were being devoted to the mobilisation of potential output and pointed to the inevitable incompleteness of a 'shadow' scheme. Higher policy was exhortative and vague rather than instructive and specific, primarily because neither the Air Ministry nor the M.A.P. officials, who realised that the activities of the industry would have to be co-ordinated by some means other than the price system, realised the immensity of the task, the nature of the information required, the techniques to be employed in its analysis, or the limitations which all this imposed on the centralisation of policy decisions. The problem was one of great novelty and complexity and its solution was to some extent hampered by the natural propensity of the firms to blame the Ministries, and the Ministries the firms, for failures which were either beyond the control of the industry or due to the deficiencies of the co-ordinating mechanisms. Finally, due weight must be given to the direct impact of the war, even in its early stages. Losses at sea, blackouts, camouflage, raw material rationing, strain and fatigue all had some effect on output.

A third factor was the failure of the local authorities in Crewe and Glasgow to provide housing. This was responsible for serious delays in the build-up of the labour force at both factories. Promises made by the Crewe Council and the Glasgow Corporation when the factories were being erected were only partially fulfilled, and in both areas the lack of accommodation for employees rapidly became the most serious problem facing the management, and one which was generally beyond their control. In May 1939 Hives had warned the Crewe Council (which had promised to erect 1000 houses by the end of 1938 and which by February 1939 had only let a contract for 100 houses) that he would remove the whole plant unless something was done, if necessary by setting up the machines at the works of sub-contractors. At this date not one house had been completed. On 12 October, T. S. Haldenby, the works manager, informed Sir Kingsley Wood that the progress of the second portion of the Crewe factory as a producing unit was almost entirely dependent on the provision of houses for an additional 2500 employees. The Crewe Council naturally had their own difficulties but they had not attempted to take full advantage of the remaining months of peace and there had been strong opposition for political reasons to the work being done by private builders. They underestimated the magnitude of the task and the cost of an adequate scheme and on 16 October the Council informed the Under Secretary of State for Air that 'without the assistance of the Air Ministry and/or the other government departments concerned there is no likelihood whatever of these houses being provided.' To the management of Rolls-Royce the Council claimed that they had had insufficient notice and knowledge of the company's requirements. Private building, which was originally to have provided 3300 houses, the majority of the total, had ceased almost entirely as a result of restrictions or shortages and an unwillingness to face the financial risk of increasing costs. The housing problem was finally tackled at the highest level and after interminable and costly delays the Air Ministry stepped in with an extensive scheme for completing the unfinished houses and extending the existing estates. In the meantime employees were billeted throughout the district.

At Glasgow the position was, if anything, a good deal worse. Nothing had been done to relieve the severe housing shortage which had slowly been developing during the thirties and it was estimated that even before the outbreak of war 12,000 houses were required. When the decision to erect the Hillington factory was taken the Glasgow Corporation had promised to erect 2500 houses, of which the first was to be ready within a year. Little progress had been made by the outbreak of war and, as at Crewe, the company was forced to take a very strong line. On 21 October the Lord Provost was informed that Rolls-Royce had decided to stop work on one-third of the factory and to move it to another town where the housing shortage was less acute. At Glasgow, as at Crewe, all housing work had stopped on the outbreak of war. Within a few weeks housing became the critical limitation on the continuing build-up of the Hillington labour force, and it was thought expedient to inform Sir Kingsley Wood that although the Hillington factory had gone ahead at great speed, its efficiency as a producing unit would be gravely hampered by the failure to provide housing. Sir Kingsley Wood was sympathetic and replied that he would do all he could to help.

At the Air Ministry the matter was investigated by F. W. Musson, who pointed out that there were 'grave difficulties' in the way of securing sanction for continued building. There was a conflict of views between the Glasgow Corporation, the Treasury and various other interested Ministries whose sanction had to be obtained. No one would act before the others and nothing was done. By March 1940 the position was serious and everyone agreed that strenuous action was required. But, as Hives told the Lord Provost of the City, Sir Patrick Dollan, there was little point in everyone agreeing that housing was necessary if no one would take an independent decision and act. It was grossly unfair that the management of Rolls-Royce, which already had its fair share of problems, should be saddled with this burden. 'Please do not refer me', Hives concluded, 'to another government department or point out that there is a shortage of building materials. You would be surprised if you knew all the shortages that we have to contend with and overcome.'

The concluding statement that 'even Crewe' had managed to do better than this was a telling point and stirred the Glasgow Corporation to take action. It was decided that the Corporation would erect 2000 houses, the control of which would be taken over entirely by the Air Ministry on their completion. This project eventually became known as the Penilee Estate. As an interim measure 350 houses on the Berry-knowes and Homfouldhead estates were made available to Rolls-Royce employees. There was considerable opposition to the scheme within the Corporation on the grounds that it was 'unfair' to local inhabitants, who had been waiting for houses for many years, to build houses for 'imported' labour brought to Glasgow for a temporary wartime project. This attitude provides as interesting example of the difficulty which some people find in weighing the relative urgency of justice and stark necessity. Fairness towards the local inhabitants in these areas was apparently a more important consideration than the fact that opposition to such proposals throughout the country might well have tipped the scales in favour of defeat. On the other hand blame should be fairly apportioned. The local politician will always take the local point of view if he and his supporters are not made aware by vigorous and convincing argument of the realities of the situation. The administrator always encounters 'unreasonable' opposition to proposals whose merit is not doubted by any intelligent individual who knows the facts. As often as not this unreasonableness must be attributed to poor communication and the inadequacy of administrative techniques. The administrator cannot expect people to respond to a situation which they do not understand, to act 'reasonably' when they do not themselves possess the knowledge of the important factors on which the administrators' reasoning is based. Up to a certain point a social group which has great confidence in an administration will accept proposals which appear to be contrary to their own interests even if unaware of the reasoning behind them. Beyond that point, however, reaction is inevitable, since the total situation to which the group is responding is different from that to which the administrator himself is responding. Unless and until these two situations are integrated, both parties will appear unreasonable to the other, and effective co-operation will not be secured. But the task of ensuring a favourable reception to housing proposals which were vitally necessary for the expansion of aero-engine production was the function of the Government and the local authorities, not the management of Rolls-Royce.

The houses on the Penilee estate began to become available in small numbers early in 1941, and it is somewhat ironical to discover that many of them were refused by employees on the grounds that the rents had been fixed too high. This was the result of an Air Ministry official's view that Rolls-Royce employees were 'richer' than others and should therefore pay higher rents. The anomalous position thus developed that employees earning similar amounts were expected to pay different rents for identical houses on different estates, depending on whether the Air Ministry or the Corporation controlled the estate. In due course the Air Ministry wisely agreed to adjust the rentals.

With housing, as with many other things, there is a wide discrepancy between 'planning' and performance. The scheme for 1500 houses was approved on 19 February 1940. None had been completed in the autumn of the same year, by which time 800 had been promised. By 6 February 1942 only 486 had been made available for occupation. This failure put a severe strain on the municipal transport of Glasgow. The position was most unsatisfactory in every way and was a constant cause of friction. The delay was attributed by Hives to the fact that the Glasgow Corporation, largely for political reasons, obstinately persisted in employing direct labour on the project instead of an experienced firm of contractors. The fine achievement of the firm of Sir Lindsay Parkinson & Co. in erecting the Hillington factory itself in record time made comparisons particularly distressing, but there was little more that the management of Rolls-Royce could do and for once Hives had to admit defeat.

The achievement of full production at Crewe and Glasgow in 1939 and 1940 was also limited by labour difficulties. Labour was not quite such a problem at Crewe as it was at Glasgow, but production at Crewe was held up by an unofficial strike, the ostensible reason for which was that girls had been put on small capstans hitherto operated by boys. These boys were on very simple machines and had had no previous experience, but their transfer was alleged to be a displacement of

'skilled labour', even though no boys had been displaced. The significant fact was that girls were not employed on this kind of work at Derby
and the management believed that the real trouble had been engineered
from Derby, whose shop stewards were trying to insist that labour
conditions at Crewe should be identical to those at Derby. This was
obviously out of the question, for, as Hives commented in a minute to
Sidgreaves, 'even if we had the desire (which we have not) we could
not possibly obtain the skilled labour in the Crewe area.' The management had no alternative but to stand firm. In a letter to Alderman Bott
of the Crewe Council, Hives pointed out that the girls were actually
more expensive than boys and made it clear that Rolls-Royce 'would
not tolerate the factory being dislocated by Trade Union rebels whom
the Unions cannot control'. The work was actually more suitable for
girls – boys soon became bored with repetitive work – and since the
unions would not allow boys over the age of 16 to be employed as
apprentices, the latter were very difficult to obtain and some were
already travelling considerable distances to work. It was estimated that
700–800 boys were required at Crewe and all the available labour from
Crewe itself had already been absorbed. The management also considered that it was unfair to start so many boys on armament work for
which there was no assured future. Another fact of some significance
was that the leading member of the strike committee was known to
have caused a strike at the Stockport works of the Fairey Company, and
was on the Air Ministry 'black list'.

The district committee of the A.E.U. endorsed the strike and advised
the National Executive of the union to endorse it. 'We claim', they said,
'that it [capstans] is a skilled job at Crewe, no matter what it is
elsewhere.' The National Executive refused to give its support, however, and Rolls-Royce declined to accept an offer by Sir Francis Joseph
to act as arbitrator, wisely insisting that the normal machinery for the
settlement of disputes should be used. On 19 April the men returned to
work unconditionally.

Some of the arguments employed by the strikers are not without
interest. They claimed that Crewe was the 'home of craftsmanship' and
that they did not intend to allow 'dilution', or to 'permit the introduction of methods employed in motor car factories'. The action of
transferring the boys was categorised as a deliberate and calculated
attempt to 'break down agreements with the men by employing
semi-skilled labour'. On the whole the customary clichés of industrial
dispute were employed but their use shows that once established, in

whatever context, human traditions and concepts develop the most powerful resistance to change. When it occurs on a large scale, involving the movement of thousands of human beings, change usually creates stress. This is more acute if the circumstances are novel and the stress will invariably find expression in actions or statements which in themselves are frequently irrational and futile. It is the task of the administrator, as well as the social historian, to discover the real origins and motivation of human conflict, but this requires the skill and capacity to lift the veil which the participants in such conflict tend to throw over their real motivations. As Warner and Low have so clearly demonstrated in their study of the industrial strike,[5] and as Alexander Leighton has shown in his analysis of social stress in the Poston relocation centre for Californian Japanese,[6] these phenomena are seldom satisfactorily explained by the simplistic cause-and-effect relationships assumed by the participants in the dispute. The purely economic, the purely legal, or the purely political explanation of such a phenomenon as a strike – a breakdown in human co-operation – though interesting and possibly informative in itself, is ingenuous because each by itself neglects so many vitally important factors. If history inevitably compels the neglect of many fascinating bypaths, it is often much the poorer for a rigid, if unavoidable, adherence to the main road. But on such subjects as an industrial strike the historian's conclusions should be regarded as a stimulus to further research rather than as a final explanation.

Glasgow also had its share of labour trouble. The Clydesiders were almost as difficult to obtain as they were to handle. The management realised that there would be strong objections from the employers in the Glasgow area to the mass transfer of labour to Hillington, but the national interest required their co-operation in achieving this. In May 1939 Hives put his request to the Glasgow employers at a luncheon in the city. He pointed out that Rolls-Royce had not asked for the Glasgow factory and that the factory would not be wasted even if there was no war, since the export drive would require modern and efficient equipment. Moreover, for every £4 spent on labour, he told them, at least £3 would be spent on materials. The reward which Rolls-Royce itself gained from all this was very small, the management fee being only a fraction of the sum which a normal rate of profit on the turnover of a factory this size would have produced.

The outcome was not encouraging. Some firms were much more co-operative than others. In the event of war the Singer Sewing

Machine Works would clearly have had to reduce production and it was agreed between the two managements that Rolls-Royce could recruit whomsoever they pleased provided that Singers retained the right to object in any particular case. This agreement was without prejudice to the right of Rolls-Royce to employ a man in the event of failure to reach agreement. Singers were of the opinion that the Hillington factory would attract most of their young men, but not many of their old employees.

The average wage in the Glasgow area was lower than in England and practically all firms had paid piece-rates with no guaranteed minimum wage. There had in consequence been a considerable out-flow of skilled men to England, and these could be retained only by paying comparable wages. The management was thus quite heavily handicapped. They had no wish to incur the displeasure of Glasgow employers by paying excessively high wages, a policy which would probably have completely stripped some firms of their labour, but the men had somehow to be found. The Air Ministry itself had not made things any easier by instructing that 'every endeavour should be made to avoid withdrawal of skilled labour from other firms in that area which are engaged in work for the defence departments.' The situation was further complicated by the existence on the Clydeside of a grade of labour known as the 'semi-skilled machinist', which did not exist in England. In some firms such as Barr & Stroud the management were able to transfer work from skilled to semi-skilled machinists without any difficulty.

No sooner had the training schemes started than the complaints began to pour in to Hillington and Derby. Many firms were particularly distressed at the loss of their key men, and wrote complaining that they were also engaged on work for one or other of the services. One firm even went so far as to set up its own scheme of inter-service priorities, declaring that the Navy, being the Senior Service, should have first choice. This dissension was unavoidable as the labour force at Hillington has to be built up as soon as possible. To avoid obligations and commitments which he knew he could or dare not fulfil, Hives deliberately refrained from joining the Scottish Employers' Federation. On 12 September he wrote a frank letter to J. B. Lang, the President of the Scottish Employers' Federation, explaining Rolls-Royce's point of view:

I am very disappointed in the attitude of the Scottish Employers; in fact, as far as I can see, it is a distinct disadvantage to us in starting a new factory being a member of the Federation. We anticipated this position when we started the Rotol Airscrew factory at Gloucester. . . . We decided then that there was no advantage in being in the Federation when we had nothing to protect, and that the attitude of the Federated Employers was only to restrict us in obtaining the necessary personnel. Now that we have built up the staff and got the factory going, we are reconsidering the question of joining the Federation.

To me it appears rather pathetic if Glasgow and district, with a population of nearly two millions, cannot find the necessary men to produce aero-engines in Scotland. If the employers take a broad view they will appreciate that we are going to train a tremendous lot of people, and I promise you we shall not squeal if men whom we have trained choose to leave us and go to another firm.

Lang's reply was apologetic, but he pointed out that although the Scottish employers wanted to co-operate in every way, 'the question of the supply of skilled labour is undoubtedly the most difficult one.' The possibility of arranging a 10 per cent levy from each firm was discussed at a later meeting, but Lang emphasised that the firms would feel happier if a limit could be placed on the number of skilled men each could be called upon to supply. Rolls-Royce was asking for 700 skilled men and there were estimated to be only 12,000 in the whole of the West of Scotland. Most of these were in heavy engineering and quite unsuitable.

In May 1940, when various factories were visited to see if labour could be obtained, it was found that 90 per cent of the labour was engaged on government work. No employer felt under any obligation to transfer men to Hillington, which made itself unpopular by paying what some employers referred to as 'exorbitant rates'. Moreover, as one of the reports on the subject stressed, 'the priority of aircraft engine work is not accepted in Glasgow'. By June the position has improved so little that H. S. Royce, who had conducted one of these surveys, suggested that the whole chassis division should be sent up from Derby. 'We should have', he added, 'people who are accustomed to working as a team . . . the advent of such a body will ginger up everybody else here very considerably.' Morale at Hillington was poor in the early stages, and when, later in the year, Major Bulman sent to Derby for a copy of a complaint against the system and the rate of scrap at Glasgow, Hives was not in the least surprised. 'We must expect,' he replied, 'that we shall get criticism in the management of any factory. But any criticism we get from outside cannot possibly approach the criticism we level against ourselves. The district is seething with communists and strikes and threats of strikes occur the whole time.'

The problems involved in building up production at Glasgow were immense and a certain amount of waste and delay was inevitable. Machine tool deliveries could not be accurately forecast, skilled technicians were reluctant to leave Derby because of the very much lower standard of living (housing and general amenities) in Glasgow, and material shortages of one sort or another caused unpredictable delays. Under the circumstances it was not surprising that some employees, to whom the stunted state of the trees was plainly visible, should have complained bitterly that the wood did not exist. Waste and inefficiency can never be completely eliminated, especially in an expanding organisation, but they are less likely to cause complaint if a convincing explanation of what is happening is given from time to time. The morale of troops who are left idle or misemployed during a war will always deteriorate unless the authorities have the sense and the courage to explain as fully as possible what is happening. This is not always possible either in an army or in industry, for there is an absolute limit to the load which any administration can bear, but the authoritarian tradition in both spheres has undoubtedly been responsible for a great deal of perverse intransigence. This unfortunately does not disappear with the conditions which originally gave rise to it. Even if the situation appears to be temporarily insoluble, the 'don't ask questions' attitude will infiltrate those who are affected by the uncertainty or conditions. The morale of an industrial organisation does not differ in any vital respect from that of any other form of association. It will deteriorate if individuals feel that their efforts are being wasted or misdirected, and the frustration which this causes will find its expression in the conventional patterns of belief prevalent in the particular section or class of the community concerned. Under conditions of rapid change in any institution or society, morale is easily destroyed unless there is both the will and the means to communicate information on what is happening and why. A partial, direct and convincing explanation is generally more effective than an impartial, complex and academic explanation which the administrator may require for his own purposes.

But although the tradition in Glasgow was, as is customary in British industry, authoritarian, there were delays and wastage which no administration could have prevented and which it would have been most difficult, and dangerous, to explain. Hives was well aware of this, and in a letter to Major Bulman written in March 1941 he replied to a serious complaint which the latter had received from a Glasgow employee via the Prime Minister:

> I have every sympathy with the writer of the letter, and a lot of his remarks are true, but our trouble is that we do not know how to avoid it. We have taken a terrific job of training raw labour, and during the building-up process it is inevitable that sections will be short of work. The fact that credit is given to the foundry for working satisfactorily gives us a certain amount of encouragement, and if it was not that we had confidence and faith that the rest of the factory would soon attain the same degree of efficiency we should give up the job.
>
> The Clydeside workers are the most difficult people in the world to handle. The fact that Hillington is a government factory they consider gives them the right to criticise it from all angles.

Though many mistakes were made, there is little doubt that the production of the first complete engine in November 1940 was an outstanding achievement. Before this Glasgow had made a very considerable contribution to the output of the other two factories by supplying parts which were in short supply. By June 1941 the target of 200 per month had been reached and by March 1942 output exceeded 400.

The control of production at Derby, Crewe and Glasgow, the continual expansion of sub-contract production, negotiations with the Ministries and services and discussions with the aircraft manufacturers by no means exhausted the scope of the management's activities but they absorbed most attention. The opportunity presented by the quiet months of 1939 and 1940 was not lost and when the first squalls of war struck in May the organisation was ready to play its part. By far the most important development during this period was the building up of a strong network of personal contacts between the senior executives of the firms and the Ministries. The mutual trust and confidence based almost invariably on personal friendship became a most valuable asset in the dark years that lay ahead. Official channels were regarded as a means rather than an end – to be used if they worked and by-passed if they didn't – and the close personal contact which was constantly maintained kept down to a minimum the misunderstandings that are bound to arise when situations get completely beyond the control of routine systems. Only on such a foundation would it have been possible to allow the constructive indulgence of mutual criticism. In such flexibility lies one of the greatest strengths of the democratic state in war.

4 Beaverbrook Raises the Voltage

In February 1940, as a result of a careful reassessment of German aircraft production made for the Chief of Air Staff, the Secretary of State for Air, Sir Samuel Hoare, decided that the British target of 2550 aircraft per month would have to be reviewed. There seemed little hope of obtaining the desired increase without a sacrifice of some of the newer machines which were scheduled to come forward in 1941. While the reformulation of this target was under discussion the attack on France began and it was soon realised that the demands which the Air Ministry had originally expected to be made on the Air Force in September 1939 would now have to be met in full. The intensity of the crisis mounted with great rapidity and within a few weeks all production had to be drastically reoriented towards supplying the insatiable needs of the R.A.F. Fighter Command had no choice but to commit the whole of its front-line strength to the defence of the corridor from Dunkerque, and, very shortly thereafter, to containing the onslaught of the Luftwaffe in the Battle of Britain.

On 10 May, Chamberlain was succeeded by Churchill with Lord Beaverbrook as Minister of Aircraft Production. Lord Beaverbrook has been well described by Commander Stephen King-Hall[1] as the man whose personality raised the voltage at the Ministry of Aircraft Production, and throughout the entire aircraft industry, to a potential far higher than it had ever carried before. Though this voltage, which no civil service system of organisation and administration had ever been designed to carry — may have blown a large number of fuses in important parts of the structure, it nevertheless ensured that for several crucial months the R.A.F. was able to tap the industrial resources of the country to a degree which would certainly not otherwise have been possible. It was also important that the industry should have a sense of participation in the conflict.

Rolls-Royce soon felt the impact of the new Minister. His aggressive realism was very much in sympathy with the outlook at Derby. There

3. Lord Beaverbrook

may have been considerable disagreement over details and methods but there was no real disharmony between Lord Beaverbrook and the management. Both disliked the mistrusted civil service routines, programmes and the ideal of careful calculation which, however admirable from the point of view of government, ignored the all-important problem of time. In April, the month before Lord Beaverbrook took office, Derby produced 204 Merlins, Crewe 185. The output of repaired engines was 130. By the end of June the output had increased to 494, that of Crewe to 345, and that of repaired engines to 292. The total output of both factories fell slightly in July and again in August, but the output of repaired engines was increased to 327 in July. The fighter squadrons which fought over Dunkerque and later in the Battle of Britain were entirely engined by the Merlin. The Hurricanes predominated, followed by the Spitfire and the Defiant. The main mark of Merlin in production at this time was the Mk. X although production of the Mk. XX was just starting at Derby. The new engines produced during the period June–October were not the engines which fought the great air battles of these months, but damaged engines had to be repaired and replaced, and, where possible the opportunity was taken during repair to introduce the latest modifications based on the experience which was being gained from intensive operation. In the rectification of faults which only came to light under service conditions the immediate liaison of the Rolls-Royce engineers at squadrons with the technical staff at Derby proved invaluable. The big output of repaired engines at this time was largely due to the efforts of R. N. Dorey, the senior engineer at Hucknall, who within a few weeks developed, on his own initiative, extensive repair and modification facilities. The whole organisation was a miracle of improvisation devoted to the single objective of getting the maximum number of aircraft back into the air in fighting trim.[2]

Three problems confronted Lord Beaverbrook. The first was to keep the front-line squadrons up to strength and, if possible, to increase their number. The second was to keep the performance of these aircraft ahead of that of the enemy. This was as much an administrative as a technical problem since the higher performance always existed on the drawing-board, on the test-bench or in the prototype. It sometimes existed in the production line. But there was a limit to the speed at which any one stage could be pushed on to the next. The greater the speed the greater the dislocation of current production and, to some extent, future output. Each stage between the drawing-board and the production line could be missed out but there was no means of calculating the risk involved in missing out one or several stages. The risk was always considerable but from time to time it had to be taken. The third problem was to ensure that present performance and present production were not gained at the expense of future performance and future production.

The first problem was purely internal in character – a question of creating the conditions under which the existing system could achieve the maximum output. This was done by imposing some restrictions and lifting others. The second problem was related to the performance of enemy aircraft and the tactical purposes for which these were being employed. Speed, altitude, endurance and firepower determined the nature and outcome of the war in the air. The third problem was a question of judging the margin, if any which the urgency of the present left for consideration of the future.

Lord Beaverbrook's first step was to concentrate production on five types of aircraft – the Wellington, Whitley, Hurricane, Spitfire and Blenheim.[3] Two of these aircraft were entirely engined by the Merlin. A similar rationalisation of engine production was proposed by the Chief Executive at the M.A.P., Sir Charles Craven, who had been brought in from Vickers. Sir Charles Craven endeavoured to persuade the industry and the Ministries that the number of engines under development and in production should be reduced to three liquid-cooled and three radial. The main liquid-cooled engines under development were the Merlin, the Griffon and the Vulture, produced by Rolls-Royce, and the Sabre, produced by Napiers. The Griffon and Vulture were both candidates for the bowler hat, but Hives would not agree at this stage to their abandonment although it was not long before he thought it advisable to allow the Vulture to drop out.

At a meeting on 22 June, attended by all the important firms in the industry, Sir Charles Craven pointed out that this was a long-term project which had no no account to interfere with current production. Hives objected to the whole proposal on the grounds that there was no point in trying to rationalise the engine programme until a 'clear-cut and stable' aircraft programme had been decided upon. But there was no possibility of this happening under Lord Beaverbrook, who was of the firm opinion that the waste which was bound to be incurred in the endeavour of each firm to produce an 'unco-ordinated' maximum output was preferable to the lower overall volume of production which a carefully planned and controlled programme might have achieved

4. The Hawker Siddeley Hurricane Mark I

without waste. In view of the serious inadequacy of the whole apparatus of centralised control at this stage of the war this was undoubtedly the correct policy. An industrial system which is producing at full blast, even if parts of it are producing in different directions, at least affords firms an opportunity to develop their maximum individual output, and it is always easier to cut down production in some sectors than to build it up in others. Beaverbrook's policy naturally implied the conclusion that the overall planning mechanism was deficient, mainly because the almost infinite complexities of the apparatus had not been appreciated. But Beaverbrook realised that the margin was so narrow that in the interests of immediate production even the relatively minor drags – physical and psychological – which the contemporary efforts to develop an apparatus of co-ordination and control had imposed on the system should be abandoned. He gave instructions that all development work was to cease (an instruction which was fortunately not obeyed indiscriminately). These instructions were all somewhat exaggerated, but their tenor was much more important than their content. Ill-judged but vigorous instructions, provided they are sufficiently specific and drastic, will often convey the necessary impression to those who have the expert knowledge to transform them into effective action.

To encourage production several restrictions were raised. On 24 May the Air Ministry asked for a works committee consisting of the Air Ministry overseer, a production officer, the firm's chief inspector and a representative of the works management to be set up with full executive powers to alter inspection procedure in the interests of maximum production. The Merlin III was given top priority at Derby. A double-shift seven-day week was introduced and except for two half-hour breaks at the change of shifts the factories were in continuous operation. The day shift was from 8.5 a.m. to 8 p.m. and the night shift from 8.30 p.m. to 7.30 a.m. Thus in a working week of 161 hours, 69 hours of overtime were worked. This pace was kept up until late in 1941 when it was decided that the effort was proving too costly in terms of sickness and absenteeism. For certain classes of labour, the hours worked exceeded the statutory maximum, but despite protests from Ministry of Labour officials, the management decided that, provided the employees agreed to do so, the effort should be made. There was no dissent. Lord Beaverbrook was informed of this decision and supported it.

On 28 May the Minister telegraphed that he had issued instructions 'to postpone all unnecessary returns forthwith'. Only output returns were to be made to the Ministry. On the following day he telegraphed that 'instructions will shortly be issued which will facilitate the financial situation for contractors and sub-contractors.' On 22 June, just after Dunkerque, when the invasion threat began to loom ahead, he wrote a characteristically melodramatic letter to Hives giving him virtually dictatorial powers in the event of a direct enemy attack:

> I appoint you Chairman of a Committee of One required to deal with Rolls-Royce properties in the case of enemy attack. You have complete authority and discretion in the organisation of R.R. output

on such terms and conditions as you desire. Your authority will also extend to all sub-contractors of Rolls-Royce whose works may be subjected to enemy attack.

Lord Beaverbrook was receptive to constructive suggestion and not in the least afraid, simply because they had come from the industry itself, of adopting suggestions which appeared reasonable. Before the blitz struck, Hives had written to Air Commodore H. Peake, a newly-elected director of the firm, who had just been appointed Director of Public Relations at the Air Ministry, commenting on the poor publicity which the services, and indirectly the products of industry, were receiving. This was having a bad effect on industrial morale. 'The men are getting bored with this war', he said; 'we have never had a single bit of information from the Air Ministry which would interest our workers.' In consequence Rolls-Royce made arrangements for the firm's own employees who had been in France to broadcast over the factory loudspeaker system and Sidgreaves suggested to the Minister that R.A.F. pilots should be brought to the factories to recount their experiences. Beaverbrook replied that he had taken note of all these suggestions and that he had appointed Beverly Baxter, M.P., in charge of publicity and propaganda.

Hives was similarly concerned with very much the same three problems at this stage of the war. His first priority was production in the Rolls-Royce group. By superhuman efforts the output of new and repaired engines and of all-important spare parts from Derby and Crewe had been stepped up. Glasgow assisted the other factories with parts but had not yet made a complete engine. But a spurt of the sort which these efforts achieved in June and July 1940 cannot be kept up indefinitely and the management was sceptical of the ability of the group to meet the demand which the M.A.P. based on the planned capacity of the airframe manufacturers. In June the group was asked to produce 3636 Merlins of all marks between August and December, and 5995 in the first six months of 1941. In July these figures were stepped up to 3639 and 6096 and in September to 3899 and 6983. At the same time the Vulture and Kestrel requirements were increased. The first figure was not excessively optimistic, the output achieved from all factories in the last five months of 1940 being 3515. But the expectations for the first six months of 1941 were far too optimistic, the output actually achieved in this period being only 4710 engines.

In view of these expectations Hives thought it expedient to raise the question of parts manufacture in the United States. Beaverbrook had his own ideas on this subject and on 28 May intervened in a drastic manner. Instructions were telephoned to Derby that a complete set of Merlin and Griffon blueprints were to be prepared for immediate transhipment to the United States. Similar instructions were also received by several other firms. This was done and the prints were collected by special train and delivered to a warship which was leaving for Canada. On 12 June Mr M. W. Wilson, the President of the Royal Bank of Canada, received the following instructions from Lord Beaverbrook. 'Please go to Washington and deliver the Rolls-Royce and Handley-Page plans to the President forthwith, intimating that you are handing them over upon my official authority and instructions with a view to their immediate use for the production of aircraft engines and frames. The rights of Rolls-Royce and Handley-Page can be left for subsequent determination and adjustment between the two countries.' A copy of these instructions was received at Derby.

As soon as this news was received at Derby, Sidgreaves gave instructions for the order to be carried out and then drafted a letter to the Minister in which he pointed out that the board was disturbed by his action. 'Whilst they appreciate that the present is not the right time to raise financial questions, nevertheless as custodians of the assets which belong to the shareholders of the Company, they feel that it is desirable to place on record the fact that in carrying out these instructions they are parting with a very valuable asset.' This letter was not sent and instead Sidgreaves and Hives requested and obtained an interview. At this meeting Lord Beaverbrook pointed out that the whole question of Merlin manufacture in the United States was under discussion at the Ministry and gave an assurance that the legitimate commercial claims of the company would not be ignored. 'Under these circumstances', he wrote a few days later, 'I would ask you to be good enough to refrain from entering into any negotiations with the American Government and to advise your American representatives accordingly.'

The chairman, Lord Herbert Scott, was particularly disturbed by this somewhat unprecedented action. On 8 June he wrote to Sidgreaves warning him that the drawings were not to be released without the consent of the board. 'Such instructions', he said, 'are our only hope of retaining any bargaining power. I believe that under recent legislation the British government have powers to authorise the U.S. Government to manufacture Rolls-Royce engines without any reference to our-

5. Sir Arthur Sidgreaves

selves. Such action would place our shareholders in an impossible position. ... Knowing something about Beaverbrook's methods he would be unscrupulous to gain a point considered to be desirable in our national interest. If, for instance, he could barter Merlins with the United States for, say, ships, guns, munitions etc., he would not hesitate to do so without any reference to ourselves or regard for our shareholders. Under such conditions we could only bow to such a decision as made for patriotic reasons. Beaverbrook holds the trump cards in the pack.' Sidgreaves was not unduly upset by this prospect. 'By the time America can produce any Merlins', he replied, 'the engine as a type will be out of date here. Quite frankly our feeling is that if their having the drawings would enable us to win the war we would willingly give them without any claim. If we lose the war it certainly won't matter about the drawings.' Sidgreaves underestimated the development potentialities of the Merlin but the remainder of his argument carried sufficient conviction.

The proposal to manufacture Merlins in the United States soon received considerable publicity in both countries. In the meantime, however, the Rolls-Royce representatives in the United States had been active in the organisation of parts, raw material and machine tool supplies. An efficient and comprehensive organisation under the control of J. McManus and Maurice Olley was set up with offices in Michigan and New York. Hives was all in favour of expanding this organisation into a great sub-contract scheme similar to that existing in England. 'I can promise you', he told the Minister, 'that you would get an infinitely better return for your money by making full use of sub-contracting in the U.S.A. and Canada to produce Merlin pieces than you will by the Ford Company attempting to make complete engines at £5,000 each.'

The question of an American Merlin licence had been raised several times even before the war by manufacturers in the United States, who had approached either McManus in New York or Colonel Darby in London. In October 1938 several enquiries had been received in London from American manufacturers who considered that the development of military aircraft in the United States was hampered by the lack of liquid-cooled engines.[4] These manufacturers had also made representations to the American Government and Colonel Darby thought that it was an opportune time to arrange a licence. Sidgreaves and Hives did not agree. 'If the American Government', wrote Sidgreaves, 'as a result of their investigations overseas, come to the conclusion that they want Rolls-Royce engines, then I would much rather they approached us than vice versa.' In November one of the directors of the Packard Company who was visiting London discussed the possibility of a licence with Colonel Darby, but nothing further came of the proposal for very much the same reasons.

After war broke out Sidgreaves wrote to McManus pointing out that Rolls-Royce was less interested than ever in granting a licence since the firm's whole effort would be fully absorbed in England. But, despite this cold water poured on every suggestion that complete engines should be made in America, McManus and Olley continued to discuss the possibility with various manufacturers who were interested in the idea. In October 1938 Olley had met the General Manager of Packards, Mr G. T. Christopher, who told him that his company was thinking of returning to the aero-engine business and suggested forming with Rolls-Royce in the United States a company similar in character to Rotols. In this event Packards would be prepared to release a proportion of their manufacturing facilities for the manufacture of Rolls-Royce products generally.

In discussing this proposal Olley could not resist a sarcastic comment on the previous organisation which Rolls-Royce had established in America after the First World War. The new company, he declared, 'would not have in it investment bankers and their stock profits, watered stock, operation from Wall Street, with overpaid officials sitting around waiting for a factory to be equipped and lined up, plus high-paid officials for selling and palatial showrooms to sit in and not sell'. Sidgreaves was neither impressed by the proposal nor stung by the sarcasm. 'In reality when we get down to it', he replied, 'we find that there are a lot of people who want to make Rolls-Royce engines, repair them and everything else so long as Rolls-Royce will do all the work.' Despite the disappointment of the Fordair project, which no doubt prompted this remark, he thought that the Ford Company would be the best equipped to undertake Merlin manufacture in the United States because of the work which their engineers had already done on behalf of their French subsidiary.

A further meeting between Maurice Olley and the Chairman of the Packard Company, Mr Gilman, took place early in December. Mr Gilman's attitude was quite co-operative, as Olley pointed out to Mr Purvis, one of the officials on the British Purchasing Commission in Washington. Gilman was ready at any time, he said, 'to put the Packard organisation to work on building Merlin engines for the Air Ministry. He is not prepared to risk the Packard Company's capital on the job, nor is he willing to sign a standard licensing agreement with Rolls-Royce or the Air Ministry which would involve the expenditure of large amounts of Packard capital without assurance of a return.'

The Packard Company wished the Air Ministry to provide all the capital as it had done for Crewe and Glasgow, and insisted on adequate protection against the financial loss which a sudden cessation of hostilities would have caused, plus a profit of 'between 10 and 15%'. Gilman fully expected that the cost of manufacture in the United States would be double that in England. He did not object to paying Rolls-Royce a royalty since this would merely be added to the cost of the engines. The Packard Company would not accept an order for less than 1000 engines and could not promise to make delivery before the end of 1940. Gilman frankly doubted if the Air Ministry would consider a proposition of this nature, especially in view of the fact that they had rejected a similar offer from his company in 1938.

In the autumn of 1939 the English management considered that its American representatives had an exaggerated idea of the importance of developing a geographically separate source of supply for complete engines. There is no doubt that the project of manufacturing complete engines in the United States had a much stronger appeal than the more mundane, but from the point of view of English production, more immediately productive scheme for parts manufacture. McManus in particular had always nurtured an ambition to redress the failure of Springfield and there is little doubt that he saw an opportunity of doing so in the American Merlin idea. Early in December S. E. Blackstone, who had gone over at Hives' request to provide Olley and McManus with an up-to-date picture of the requirements of the English factories, especially in machine tools for Crewe and Glasgow, reported back that both of them were disappointed that the British Government was not going ahead. It was not easy, he said, to satisfy them 'that there were no urgent requirements for parts beyond a few which were considered to be vulnerable to air attack, and that our job at present is merely exploratory, to find potential sources for some of the major items such as steels, aluminium castings and forgings, machining larger parts etc.' Maurice Olley, whose 1914–18 experiences in the United States were still very vivid, was convinced that a complete Merlin would have to be manufactured sooner or later. He had a poor opinion of the only other liquid-cooled in-line engine then being manufactured in America and considered that though other engines were under development they would be unlikely to appear in time, or to be superior to the Merlin when they did.

The reasons for the English management's continued opposition to the idea were not insubstantial. In a memorandum to McManus, Sidgreaves summarised the main argument.

On the question of going further with Packard the position is really quite definite that I am not interested in forming any more companies. If Packard wants to make Rolls-Royce engines the only way will be for Packard to build our machines under licence and for the necessary personnel to come over here to study the job from A to Z so that they can go back to America fully equipped with all the information to enable them to produce . . . We cannot spare any more personnel for technical educational purposes.

This reply clearly showed that there was no immediate prospect of building complete Merlins in the United States on the Company's own initiative, but even this did not extinguish the enthusiasm of the Rolls-Royce representatives in the U.S.A. Both continued to discuss various proposals with industrialists and with the senior technical officials of the U.S. Army Air Force and the U.S. Navy. On 2 March McManus cabled a request that Derby should supply the War Department with two Merlin engines of the latest type. This request emerged from a visit which he and Olley had paid to Brigadier-General G. H. Brett and Rear-Admiral Towers at Washington in an attempt to interest the United States service chiefs directly in the Merlin as an engine for American fighter aircraft. The performance of American fighter aircraft in 1939 was notoriously inferior to that of the aircraft of the major European powers. But before the Army or Navy could give a production order for any engine it had to clear the Wright Field acceptance tests (equivalent to the Air Ministry type tests) and General Brett was very keen to obtain the latest mark of engine for this purpose. These tests were constructive in character and he was prepared to allow Rolls-Royce engineers to be present, an exceptional privilege at that time. Maurice Olley kept a diary of these events and has subsequently summarised the outcome of the talks as follows. 'General Brett was interested and strongly advocated the development of the Merlin in parallel with the Allison engine for fighter aircraft. Towers, on the other hand, said that the Navy would be interested in putting water-cooled engines into their aircraft on the same day that they installed air-cooled power plants in their submarines.'

Unfortunately this request was not considered as the forerunner of a serious proposal. Sidgreaves thought that the Americans were anxious merely to obtain technical information and he decided that the United Kingdom could not spare two of the latest engines for this purpose. He replied to Olley that the pressure of Air Ministry orders made it impossible to supply two engines. An earlier request transmitted through the American Embassy in London had met with a similar response.

In April Sidgreaves informed McManus that the question of supplying the War Department with sample Merlins in exchange for Allison engines, in which Rolls-Royce was not interested, had become a 'purely political' problem which was being handled by the Air Ministry. On the 9th instructions were received to release two engines and McManus was informed accordingly. Before this the only Merlin in the United States was a specially finished dummy engine which had been sent over as an exhibit for the World's Fair. Until the new engines arrived this engine, which was entirely unsuited for the purpose, was in great demand as a sample.

In June the whole situation in the United States became most confused. The question of producing the Merlin and the choice of manufacturer had been taken completely out of Rolls-Royce's hands and Sidgreaves was under the impression that a large order had been given to the Ford Company. The New York *Herald Tribune* reported on 20 June that Lord Beaverbrook had awarded a contract for 6000 engines to the Ford Company. In Washington it was suspected that this confusion arose as a result of manoeuvring between different manufacturers in the automobile industry, all of whom wanted the publicity which attached to the manufacture of a Rolls-Royce product. A flood of confused cables and letters descended upon Derby from McManus, who, as Sidgreaves later had occasion to point out to Lord Beaverbrook, was 'actuated by an excess of zeal' on Rolls-Royce's behalf. McManus was an intensely jealous guardian of the company's interests and he suspected every manufacturer in the industry of seeking to exploit the goodwill of the name. There was some truth in this but McManus was an unduly ardent collector of ulterior motives. He was consequently inclined to prejudice negotiations by an over-legalistic caution and on several occasions his enthusiasm caused considerable difficulty both in the United States and England.

Full credit must nevertheless be given to this redoubtable trio, McManus, Maurice Olley and L. G. Ringholz for the immense energy and drive which they put into the organisation of the Michigan company. Through its early arrival on the scene and because of

McManus's appreciation of the fact that small companies were an excellent source of supply – the larger companies having confined work to their own factories in order to justify plant expansion and capital assistance – this company was able to maintain a flow of small tools and parts to the Rolls-Royce and Rotol factories at a time when they could not possibly have been obtained elsewhere.

Mr Kurt Knudsen, then chairman of General Motors, whom President Roosevelt had brought in to control the Office of Production Management, was primarily responsible for the allocation of the Merlin blueprints and for the approval of any major defence contracts involving the United States Government. On 21 July Maurice Olley visited him at his home to discuss the progress of the Merlin scheme. By this time it had been definitely decided that the Ford Company would not undertake the contract. The general opinion in Washington was that although the Ford Company might have been prepared to build an engine which was similar to the Merlin, the Merlin itself was too intricate a piece of machinery for Ford production methods.[5] One of the main factors responsible for Henry Ford's opposition to the idea was that the contract was with the British as well as the United States Government. He was still of the opinion that any direct orders for Britain should not be handled by his Dearborn works. He did not – in company with many others in June 1940 – entertain very sanguine hopes about the prospects of British survival.

As soon as the Ford Company had reached this decision the Packard Company, with whom negotiations had been carried on concurrently by the British Purchasing Commission and the Defence Finance Corporation, was offered the contract and accepted it. The first order was for 9000 engines, of which 6000 were for the British Government and 3000 for the American Government. The first serious offer to the Packard Company was made by Mr Knudsen on 24 June when he asked the chairman, Mr Gilman, and the chief engineer, Colonel Vincent, if the Packard Company would consider such an order. The proposal was favourably received and on 26 June a conference on the Merlin 28 was held at the Office of Production Management in Washington. It was decided that the engine was to be duplicated exactly except for pressure-type carburettors, and U.S. standard vacuum pumps, fuel pumps, generators, tachometer drives and other miscellaneous items. On 27 June Mr Knudsen authorised Colonel Vincent to organise a separate engineering division and to proceed at full speed without waiting for contract sanction. The Merlin blueprints, but not the parts which the Ford Company had produced, were taken over the following day. Both capital and current production costs were to be provided by the British and American Governments in the proportion of two-thirds to one-third. The price of the first 1500 engines was fixed on the basis of cost plus a fixed fee, after which a new fixed price was to be negotiated for the remainder. In the event of failure to agree, the cost plus fixed fee principle was to remain in operation. The two governments acquired an option to purchase a further 10,000 engines in two batches of 5000 within six months of the completion of the existing contract. It was estimated that the order would cost the British Government about £30,000,000, a staggering sum in 1940 real values, and that the first Packard engines could be expected in the summer of 1941.

As soon as this agreement between the two governments was finalised it became obvious that the Packard organisation would require technical assistance of the very highest quality – precisely the type of individual who could least be spared from England. Earlier on in 1940 Lord Beaverbrook had insisted that he would not permit any technicians to leave England for any purpose whatever and he had opposed a commendable suggestion that the Bristol and Rolls-Royce development sections should be transferred to Canada (where it was proposed that they should combine) on precisely these grounds. It was nevertheless imperative that Packard be given technical assistance in the interpretation of Rolls-Royce blueprints and production technique and that the closest possible liaison between the two companies should be maintained. On 18 July Olley cabled Derby that 'Gilman regards Packards as started today'. This was followed by a request for eight men and for the latest Griffon drawings since Packards wished to plan the layout of their Merlin line so that it could easily be transferred to the production of Griffons in due course.

On 8 July Sidgreaves asked Lord Beaverbrook for information on certain important points of procedure. He wanted to know whether or not the American engines should be completely interchangeable with the British, what authority Packards would have to depart from British drawings and material specifications and whether they would employ British or American accessories. He also asked whether in the early stages Packards would supply parts to Great Britain as each new factory in England had done before it was ready to produce complete engines. All these questions had to be answered before the three Rolls-Royce representatives, Lt.-Colonel T. B. Barrington (chief designer of the Aero

Division), J. E. Ellor (development engineer of the Aero Division) and J. M. Reid (production engineer), left for America. Sidgreaves informed Lord Beaverbrook that he was bringing them to see him before they left. 'Although', he added, 'this is a direct contract from the British government to the Packard Company and therefore Rolls-Royce carry no responsibility for the placing or the execution of the contract, it is inevitable that the success of the undertaking will depend on Rolls-Royce and it is certain we shall be blamed for any failure or difficulties which may arise.' All these points were satisfactorily settled by the Minister and the three engineers arrived in America on 2 August to find that the Packard Company, under the immediate direction of the Chief Engineer, Colonel Vincent, had already shown a good deal of initiative and had made considerable progress. By comparison with the Fordair scheme this was a propitious portent.

The production of the Merlin engine in the United States was a very considerable undertaking and the relatively short period between the signing of the contract on 3 September 1940 and the production of the first engine in September 1941 was, by any standard, an outstanding achievement. The company planned to produce its first hand-made engine by 20 March 1941, and its first assembly-line engine by 20 July. At the time Hives considered that this was a most optimistic forecast. On 10 October in a report to Lord Beaverbrook he commented on the satisfactory progress being made at the Packard plant. 'The target which Packards have set themselves for delivery is far better than anything we have been able to achieve, but we are not going to say it cannot be done. We want to give them all the help and encouragement we can.' The Packard estimate was not inordinately optimistic, and had the delivery of machine tools been up to anticipations the target would probably have been achieved. As at Glasgow the main limiting factor in the build-up of production was the output of gears. Quantity production on the British scale was achieved by April 1942 (510 engines) and in 1943 production averaged 1024 engines a month. In 1944 the stupendous total of 23,169 engines was produced, an average output of 1930 a month, a figure only some 300 engines less than the average total monthly production of the entire Rolls-Royce group in the same period. The average cost per engine reached a minimum of $11,080 in January 1944 and maintained an overall average of just over $12,000, a figure which did not increase despite the increasing complexity of the latest types of Merlin. In all, 55,000 engines were produced at the Packard plant in Detroit at a total cost of $691,800,000 (including capital assistance provided by both governments). Of this total over 25,000 Merlins were supplied to aircraft manufacturers in Great Britain or other parts of the Empire. These figures pay their own tribute to the productive capacity and flexibility of the industrial system of the democracies in time of war.

Though the detailed history of the development of Merlin production in the United States belongs properly to the economic history of the Packard Company[6] rather than Rolls-Royce, except in so far as the U.S. production and the relationship between the two companies affected M.A.P. and Rolls-Royce policy, some of the details are of considerable interest and provide significant comparisons.

As soon as Barrington, Ellor and Reid arrived in the United States they suggested that Packards produce the two-piece cyclinder block which had been developed on prototype engines at Derby. This block has been developed to overcome the coolant-leakage difficulties which were anticipated, and which did not fail to materialise, when the decision was taken to use a Kestrel-type head on the Merlin II in order to get a satisfactory engine into production. The Merlin 61 was the first production engine to employ the two-piece block at Derby. In consequence the Packard Merlins, which appeared before the Merlin 61, were the first to incorporate this development. This proposal was acceptable to all concerned at Packards but it was not long before it was realised that the engines produced for the U.S. Government would have to be different – in order to conform to U.S.A.A.F. requirements – from those produced for the British Merlins of the same mark. The first major task was to convert British drawings to the third-angle projection type used in the United States. In addition specifications had to be established for the finish of all parts and placed upon the drawings. This has never been done in England because personnel at Derby had long been accustomed to the required finishes. For mass production these had to be clearly defined.

All this work occupied 75 men continuously for four months. A total of 2500 drawings was involved and 125,000 prints had to be issued before production could start. The sectioning of sample castings obtained from England revealed that in some cases the drawings did not correspond exactly. These discrepancies had to be cleared up before final production specifications were issued. In addition the designs of some cast aluminium parts had to be revised and the patterns reworked. One of the biggest tasks was the duplication of British Whitworth threads. Not only did Packard find it impossible to

obtain all the engineering information which they required to repro-
duce these threads; they also discovered that all the American firms
making taps, dies and thread gauges were already overloaded with
work. There was no alternative but to enlist the aid of non-specialist
sources in the automobile industry, and this was done.

Practically all the jigs, tools and fixtures required were special and
the majority of them could not be designed until the production studies
had been completed and the operations agreed. A total of 60,000
gauges, tools and fixtures were constructed. In the initial stages, when
the project did not have a high defence priority rating, production was
held up by a shortage of the 3575 machine tools required to achieve
the desired rate of production. Only 10 per cent of the existing tools in
the Packard plant were suitable for Merlin production.

In all this work the three Rolls-Royce engineers performed an
exacting and prodigious task. Their advice was constantly sought and
there is no doubt that had the company sent over men of lesser calibre
Packards would not have produced their first production engine in
1941. Had the Packard Company acted earlier on Hives' strong recommendation that they should also send some of their best men to
England in the early stages, the burden of technical liaison would not
have had to be borne entirely by the Rolls-Royce men. Colonel
Barrington's death in 1943, shortly after returning from a visit to
England, cannot be dissociated from the immense strain which this
vast undertaking must have imposed on him.

A large number of purely engineering problems had to be settled,
many of them arising out of long-established differences in British and
American engineering practices. Their solution was further complicated by the necessity to produce two types of the same mark of
engine.[7]

As Colonel Vincent frankly admitted, the task of producing an
aero-engine such as the Merlin taxed the resources of his company to
the uttermost. 'At the time when our contracts with the British and U.S.
Governments were entered into no one in the United States had or
could have had any definite idea of the magnitude of the undertaking,
which is another way of saying that it would have been impossible to
establish accurate production schedules at this time. We know that the
suggested schedules were optimistic but we were willing to accept
them.' Such a clear appreciation of the relationship between programme and uncertainties did not exist in the United Kingdom.

The officials of the Ford Company should be exempted from this criticism since their experience of the Fordair project had provided them with a clear idea of the difficulties involved. It is all the more to the credit of the Packard Company that its management was not daunted by the unknown. From a financial point of view the undertaking was virtually risk-free since the British and American governments defrayed the entire capital cost as well as production costs; but the engineering risk was considerable.

The production of the Merlin in the Detroit works of the Packard Company marks the final stage in the development and application of quantity production techniques to the manufacture of the Merlin engine. Though not in any way under the direct control of the Rolls-Royce management the Packard Company was able to draw on the experience accumulated at Derby, Crewe, Glasgow and Fords and to avoid some of the pitfalls which had been discovered in each successive stage of expansion. The Packard management was not saddled with the problem of erecting or equipping a completely new factory, however. The existing floor space was adequate for machining purposes and only an office block and assembly shop had to be specially built. Flow-production methods were developed even further than at Glasgow and Fords to achieve an output of three engines per hour. This set twenty minutes as the maximum time allowed for any single operation. Operations requiring longer than this were broken down and carried out by machines specially designed to complete the process within this limit. The engines were carried on a mechanical conveyor which moved at forty feet per hour to produce 1800 engines a month at full production. This example of the mass production of quality might well have impressed even so exacting a critic as Sir Henry Royce.[8]

The Packard scheme was more complete than Crewe from the point of view of dependence on sub-contracting but less complete than Glasgow.[9] It was not, especially in the later stages, absolutely dependent on Derby from the point of view of design and development. The Packard Company carried out independent development work and several interesting and important modifications were made to the design of the American-built Merlin. Some of these, such as the Stromberg carburettor and silver-lead indium bearings, were adopted as soon as the Packard Merlin went into production. Others, such as the planetary supercharger drive mechanism (developed as a result of independent study of the two-stage supercharger problem) and modifications to the coolant pump and the camshaft drive, were made while the engine was in production.

Though all these contributions were most valuable, the outstanding improvements to the engine, which kept it in the forefront until the end of the war, resulted from the intensive development work carried on at Derby. These developments were immediately made available in the United States. In view of the intricate nature of the work, and the long familiarity with an engine which is the most necessary foundation for successful development work, the surprising thing is that the Packard organisation was able, being so fully occupied with the immense task of production, to carry out any design work or technical development.

The Packard project was impressive in scope and its eventual contribution to the war effort very great,[10] but in the crucial years of 1940 and 1941 the supply of parts and raw materials from the United States was of far greater immediate significance and the build-up of production in the English factories was particularly dependent on the supply of machine tools, ball-bearings and certain other 'bottleneck' items. In 1941 a complete Merlin in a front-line aircraft in North Africa, Burma or the United Kingdom was worth an almost infinite number of Merlins in the process of production at Detroit. In this respect the work of the British Purchasing Commission and of the small company which McManus had incorporated in Michigan under the name Rolls-Royce was of great importance. In the initial stages the Michigan company acted as an agent for both Rolls-Royce and Rotols and showed great enterprise in discovering and harnessing sub-contracting capacity. After the passage of the Lend-Lease Act direct purchases with British funds could no longer be made and Rolls-Royce Incorporated there-upon became a direct contractor to the American Government. The volume of orders handled eventually became quite substantial. As far as Merlin production was concerned the most important work of the Michigan company lay in the technical assistance which it gave to companies such as the Wyman-Gordon Company with whom a large order for crankshaft forgings had been placed soon after the outbreak of war. Material specifications were often a source of difficulty in obtaining supplies of steels, forgings and other similar products from the United States and in this respect the work of Dr J. M Lessels, a metallurgist on the staff of the Massachusetts Institute of Technology, whose services Rolls-Royce retained as a consultant, was of great value. The Michigan company provided a headquarters from which all these variegated operations could be carried out and also performed the important task of reporting to England week by week the progress of machine tool and raw material orders. This information made possible much more accurate predictions of the rate of increase in production at the various factories in the group.

5 Contrary to Official Recommendations

A problem which occupied a great deal of the management's interest during the Battle of Britain was armament. For very different reasons Rolls-Royce had once previously become interested in armament manufacture during the First World War when Claude Johnson endeavoured unsuccessfully to interest the authorities in the production of the Madsen machine gun. The firm's interest was again aroused in 1939. Rolls-Royce engineers who had visited the Hispano gun factory in France, the Oerlikon factory in Switzerland, the Royal Ordnance factory at Woolwich and the armaments section at the Air Ministry were struck by the advances which had been made on the continent compared with the slow progress of British factories. They were appalled by the complete dependence of the United Kingdom on foreign sources of supply for certain types of gun. 'Our impression', they reported, 'after seeing the continental gun factories, compared with Enfield, is that it is long overdue for us as a nation to be employing more brains on armaments.' The management had no intention of investing capital in the production of guns, but it was decided to establish a small section under the direction of an armaments expert, S. M. Viale, with the object of designing a 40 mm cannon and a 0.5 inch machine gun suitable for aircraft work. Rapid progress was made and the barrel and breech-block of the cannon were ready for testing within a few weeks of the outbreak of war. The first prototype was fully completed in November.

Rolls-Royce was not able to arouse the interest of the Air Ministry in either of these projects but the Admiralty admired the gun sufficiently to order a small quantity to be made by the British United Shoe Machinery Company. The development section was kept in being at Derby and work on the two guns continued.

In May and June 1940 it soon became apparent that superiority in the air depended on superior firepower as well as on the superior performance of aircraft. German fighters were employing a combination of cannon and machine guns which conferred a distinct advantage under certain conditions and the view was widely held, even in the public press, that the calibre of British aircraft armament would have to be increased as soon as possible. On 23 June, in a letter to Lord Beaver-brook, Hives stressed the view that the provision of 0.5 inch machine guns for aircraft and 40 mm cannon for ground defence were projects of the greatest immediate importance. The Air Ministry had hoped to obtain a 0.5 inch machine gun from a Belgian company but the capture of this factory by the Germans eliminated this possibility completely. There was no time to be lost and Rolls-Royce promised to have the first machine gun ready within six weeks. Work on the machine gun had started on 15 February 1940.

The firm had little experience of gun production, but, as Hives pointed out to the Minister, 'against that you have the record that whatever the Rolls-Royce Company have taken up they have made a success of it.' Early in July Sir John Salmond visited Derby and discussed the development of the guns. Nothing came of his visit however and only two prototypes of the machine gun were finally produced. This was partly because of a lack of enthusiasm amongst the armament officials at the Air Ministry and partly because it was felt that the management of Rolls-Royce should not have their attention distracted from aero-engine production in any way. When Hives approached Lord Beaverbrook with the details of the Admiralty pro-posal in August he agreed on condition that the Admiralty took over the development of the gun. 'I want Rolls-Royce to produce aero-engines – nothing but aero-engines', he replied. It was also considered by some senior officers, amongst whom was Air Chief Marshal Sir Hugh Dowding, that the muzzle velocity of the gun was too low. Later in the same month a number of Admiralty officers visited Derby and showed great interest in the cannon. Rolls-Royce was not in a position to undertake the production of this gun, but it was decided to carry out proofing tests, to proceed with its development at Derby and that the Admiralty should order the special tools required for production from the United States and arrange the necessary production facilities. In due course the development of the automatic fire apparatus for this gun was handed over to Messrs Nash & Thompson.

A brochure on the gun was submitted to the Admiralty on 13 August and the British United Shoe Machinery Company was persuaded to accept responsibility for limited production. This company was unwil-ling to control a sub-contract organisation but agreed to divert some of

6. The Rolls-Royce Prototype 40mm Cannon

its own production facilities. The M.A.P. finally agreed to allow Rolls-Royce to continue development work and provide technical parentage. Although the gun was eventually produced in some quantities and proved an excellent weapon for the motor torpedo boat type of craft, the project was not a success. A certain amount of development work continued almost until the end of the war but the gun did not prove acceptable to the Air Force or the Army.[1] From many points of view the Bofors was considered to be a superior weapon. Both the management and the engineers in the gun division were discouraged by the reception which the firm's endeavours in this field had been given and in 1943 it was decided to discontinue armament work. The knowledge that Rolls-Royce's entry into the gun design field had acted as a powerful stimulus to the older firms was some small consolation.[2]

In September and October the bombing became much more severe although, surprisingly, no serious raids were attempted on Derby or Crewe throughout 1940. The Hillington factory was bombed on 24 July but the damage was superficial and there were no casualties. This encouraged an illusion of comparative security in towns which had seen no visible signs of the enemy or the destruction which he was causing and in consequence the management had great difficulty in persuading employees to take drastic measures or to work an abnormal amount of overtime. Hives complained to Lord Beaverbrook that conflicting statements issued by various Ministries were making the task of management unnecessarily difficult. He quoted the following examples to the Minister:

(1) The Prime Minister states the Air Force is growing stronger every day.
(2) The Minister of Aircraft Production states that he has been able to replace all casualties by the repair of aircraft.
(3) The Minister of Labour states that the workers should have rest periods.
(4) The Minister of Health complains because we are working our female dilutees more than the recognised hours.
(5) The medical profession will always say a man requires a holiday if they know he is working at Rolls-Royce.

We are spending our time trying to explain that the Ministers don't mean what they say and that there is a dangerous shortage of aircraft. We are not at all impressed by the M.A.P.'s propaganda in the factories. A Conservative M.P. does not impress our workers one little bit. We could do infinitely better ourselves. It needs someone who understands the psychology of the workers. ... We quite understand that the national propaganda has got to be different in character from factory propaganda, and factory propaganda will have to be adapted to suit its own peculiar conditions. As we are fighting for the national freedom of the individual we cannot use force, so we must rely on the right kind of appeal and our contention is that so far this has not been made.

He suggested, as an example of the type of appeal which would have some effect, that some of the women who had been bombed out in London should be sent round the aircraft factories. These suggestions did not fall on deaf ears. Beaverbrook replied that he was grateful for this criticism which he considered would have a most beneficial effect. A few days later Hives visited London to discuss engine policy with him and saw some of the results of the bombing for himself. On his return to Derby he immediately arranged for four members of the Shop Committee to go up to London by car.

In a report to the board, Hives summarised the results of his discussions with the Minister. The Bristol factory had been hit and badly damaged and in consequence Lord Beaverbrook had decided that the main factories should disperse as much as possible to reduce their vulnerability. The R.A.F. was now even more dependent than before on the Rolls-Royce factories. It did not take the Government long to discover however that the psychological effects of bombing were both more dangerous and less predictable than the physical. In 1940 the Luftwaffe was concentrating all its power on defeating the R.A.F. and on destroying the morale of the British people. Industrial destruction was fitted into this pattern wherever possible and convenient. 'Results have shown', said Hives, 'that bombing has not destroyed any considerable number of machine tools. The thing it does destroy is the morale of the workers, and this is very difficult to restore. . . . Our instructions are to disperse as much as we can. . . . I spent two hours with Lord Beaverbrook and he showed me all the confidential reports. There is one thing which has no need to be kept secret as far as we are concerned, and that is that we are not producing nearly enough engines. We must produce more and we want them at once.'

The great increase in production which had been achieved at both factories in the summer and autumn was not maintained during the last few months of the year, the total output declining from 778 in October to 606 in December. It had recovered to 920 by March 1941, but the average in the first six months of 1941, during which the first complete engines from Glasgow began to come in, remained at 785. The total number of engines produced during this period was 4710, the total number absorbed into airframes 4137. In February, however, output was exceeded by absorption for the first time. This figure (785) was 300 in excess of the output expected in the last pre-war programme (11 August 1939), 129 in excess of that demanded by the 29 March 1940 programme, 559 below that demanded by the 26 July programme and 485 below that expected in a programme issued on 7 March 1941 (for which the calculations were presumably made before February). The error in these estimates was thus substantial. This was partly due to the change in type from the Merlin III and X to the Merlin XX[3] and to the effort which was being made at Derby to bring the Vulture into production. The M.A.P. programmes were little more than extravagant hopes which made little allowance for the many vicissitudes of war production and there was no escaping the fact that the production of the Merlin XX was at a dangerously low level.

Hives was well aware of this and he immediately set about analysing the causes of the failure. The M.A.P. programmes were based largely on the firm's own estimates of production and Rolls-Royce officials had been persuaded to set these unduly high towards the latter part of 1940. The methods of the M.A.P. were well known and it was felt that since their programmes would make little difference to the output actually obtained, if the Air Ministry and M.A.P. insisted on unrealistic and optimistic estimates, the easiest thing to do was to provide them! Lord Beaverbrook himself was largely responsible for the insistence of the M.A.P. that unrealistic programmes should not be altered downwards. On 3 December 1940 he had told the heads of the various production departments that the programmes must stand, 'damage or no damage'. This statement shows quite clearly that he was using the programme as a psychological device rather than as an instrument of measurement or control. As a psychological device the target programme has grave weaknesses, especially when, as was the case in December 1940, the psychological maxima have already been reached. There were no responsible officials either at the M.A.P. or in the firms who did not realise that a maximum effort was demanded. But there were many people who, for a variety of reasons, had no very clear idea of how this maximum effort could best be directed.

In a report on the general state of engine production throughout the group written on 17 December 1940 Hives maintained that output was still in excess of absorption, although he expected the latter to increase. 'According to Air Ministry programmes', he added, 'we are several hundred engines in debt, but from experience we know that all Air Ministry programmes are at least 30 per cent higher than is ever obtained.' In due course Lord Beaverbrook agreed to scale the programmes down to figures which were more reasonable. The production target of all types of aircraft by December 1941 laid down in the October 1940 programme was reduced from 2782 to 2221 per month. The bombing of the B.T.-H. magneto works, which had considerable repercussions on the output of complete engines, was mainly responsible for this decision.

Late in December Hives visited Sir Patrick Hennessy, Lord Beaverbrook's personal assistant at the M.A.P., to discuss the whole subject of programming. As a result of this discussion he again recommended that Rolls-Royce should supply the aircraft manufacturers directly.

> Everyone knows that the collection of figures which are sent out in the present Air Ministry provisioning programmes don't mean anything. We take no notice of them.
>
> The only way we are able to meet the varying demands as regards types and quantities is by direct contact with the consumer (aircraft constructor) which is confirmed by our own representatives who are permanently resident at each of the aircraft constructors. Our proposal is that this method should be officially recognised by the M.A.P. and adopted as a basis of engine production programmes. All we ask is that Rolls-Royce should receive every month from each of the aircraft constructors who are using our engines a statement showing their requirements. ... Looking at the figures for the number of Rolls-Royce engines required this year which are on the Air Ministry programme, it is certain that we can never produce them by a considerable margin. At the same time we are confident that we can meet all the requirements.

The Ministry would not agree to this proposal since it would have meant abandoning the comforting illusion that the programmes controlled the output of engines. There were other good reasons for requiring the engine firms to produce an output in excess of that which the demands of aircraft constructors alone would have brought forth,[4] but these do not seem ever to have been clearly set out for the benefit of those who were endeavouring to operate under the programme regime.

The real reasons for the failure of production to rise must be sought elsewhere. When, early in 1940, the Air Staff had discussed the trends of German production and development they had reached the conclusion that the R.A.F. was in danger of losing the technical superiority, especially of its fighters, with which it entered the war and which had proved of such immense importance during the Battle of Britain. It was felt that this could be maintained only by bringing into production new *types* of higher-powered engine and in this respect the Rolls-Royce Vulture and the Napier Sabre were looked upon as the logical successors to the Merlin. The Vulture was intended for the Avro Manchester twin-engined heavy bomber and the Sabre for the Hawker Typhoon. The Vulture was abandoned before its development had been completed because of Hives' insistence that Rolls-Royce should concentrate on the Merlin and Griffon. The Sabre's development was so slow that when it finally did come into production the purpose for which it had originally been designed had been fulfilled by other engines. Throughout 1941 the Air Ministry and the M.A.P. were unable to formulate a clear policy on these two engines and at one stage it was uncertain whether the development of the Sabre would be handed over to Rolls-Royce or the Glasgow factory turned over to the production of the Sabre. Both proposals were seriously considered.

In June 1940 Hives advised Sir Wilfrid Freeman that it would be in the best interests of the R.A.F. to produce the Merlin rather than the Vulture or Sabre. His main argument was that these 24-cylinder engines were not installationally interchangeable with the Merlin and that if the factory producing either engine were to be bombed the Merlin could not be used in their place, with the result that new aircraft would be grounded without engines. As a result of the order suspending development work after Dunkerque and the impairment in the co-ordination of policy on design and development between the M.A.P. and the Air Ministry which took place under Lord Beaverbrook, the situation became increasingly confused towards the end of 1940. This confusion produced a crop of wild schemes and rumours which did not disappear until the Joint Production and Development Committee under the chairmanship of Sir Henry Tizard was established. The return of Sir Wilfrid Freeman from the M.A.P. to the Air Ministry, where he was no longer able to maintain such close contact with the firms, had a great deal to do with the blurring of policy which was evident at this time.

On 9 October the chairman, Lord Herbert Scott, wrote to Sidgreaves expressing great concern over the propaganda which was being developed about the relative merits of the Sabre and the Vulture. He foresaw the danger that the authorities, the Air Force, and the pilots would become divided into two camps and suggested that this would not be in the best interests of the war effort. He concluded with a somewhat drastic suggestion. 'From a national and company point of view we should do all we can to prevent Napier going into full production. . . . It is a dangerous policy to change horses (engines) crossing a river.' Lord Herbert Scott suspected that the boost which was being given to the Sabre had financial implications and his long association with Rolls-Royce and his experience of the type of inter-company politics which characterised the First World War inclined him to take a somewhat narrow point of view on the subject.

Hives needed no reminding of the dangers in the Sabre/Vulture policy, but he refused to lend his authority to political manoeuvres of this description, following the clear precedent which Claude Johnson had established in the First World War. 'I thought', he commented in a minute to Sidgreaves, 'it had been accepted that the only thing that mattered was to win the war and that the question of commercial prestige was to be forgotten in the present struggle. Considering that the country is purchasing thousands of aero-engines from the U.S.A. I do not see how we could justify any endeavour to prevent the Sabre engine going into production. . . The answer to the Sabre is for us to show that the Vulture is the better engine. That is the only thing that counts in the end.'

The problem was nevertheless of national proportions since the decision involved the allocation of the resources of a major part of the aero-engine capacity in the country, in particular the No. 1 Shadow Group which was about to complete its Pegasus and Mercury contracts. The Centaurus, Griffon, Sabre and Vulture were the candidates for production in these factories and in August 1941 it was decided to allot 75 per cent of the capacity of the group to the Sabre at a conversion cost alone of over £3 million. The Vulture was rejected because of its failure on the Manchester and the Griffon because of its relatively undeveloped state and the burden which the technical parentage of an outside group of factories would have imposed on the Rolls-Royce management. Within a few months the failure of the Sabre engine made it necessary to reverse this decision and switch the whole group on to the Bristol Hercules engine.

Hives took a serious view of these possibilities and in October 1940 he expressed his doubts in a lengthy memorandum to Lord Beaverbrook which, despite the accuracy of its predictions, must have caused the Minister some amusement. Unfortunately it did not have the desired effect.

> During our 25 years experience of building aero-engines we have watched the rise and fall of Air Ministers and the coming and going of senior R.A.F. officers, and our long experience has enabled us to formulate a correction factor for the Civil Service. Consistently every few years we have been faced with some wonderful new engine which was the last word in performance and efficiency and which made it only a matter of time before Rolls-Royce would be out of business. There have been times when we have been so impressed

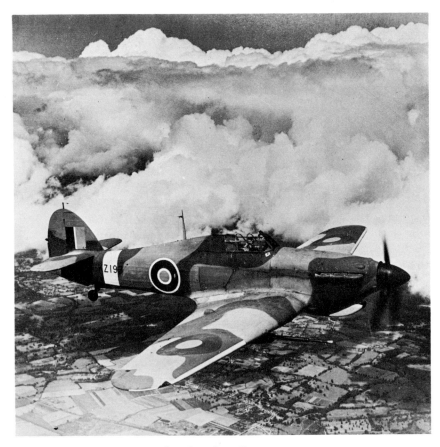

7. A Hurricane fitted with Rolls-Royce 40mm cannon

with the information that we have believed it ourselves, but fortunately we have never believed it to the extent of dropping the substance and chasing the shadow.

It has been embarrassing at times because some of the senior technical officials at the Air Ministry have backed these projects to an extent far beyond what was justified and proved by subsequent results. *Most of the Rolls-Royce successes have been achieved when we have acted contrary to the official recommendations.*

Hives felt that he could place little faith in reports that wonderful new aircraft were about to take the air. 'We know the position as regards fighter aircraft, and it is positively certain that the only machines we shall have to fight the Germans with in 1941 are the Hurricane and Spitfire.' The policy should be, he suggested, to make these two aircraft 'as good as we know how to make them'. The Hurricane with the Merlin XX had a greatly improved performance and the output of the Merlin XX could be greatly increased if orders for the Merlin III were reduced. In conclusion he argued that it was absurd to expect any contribution from the Sabre Typhoon during 1941. 'A Rolls-Royce quotation is that one machine in the air is worth an infinite number on the drawing board, in the workshops or on the ground.'

Beaverbrook replied immediately in a short note saying that, as usual, he welcomed criticism 'bearing in mind always the need for brevity and in terms that will enable us to reach conclusions rather than delve into reasons for errors and mistakes in the past.' A short while later he replied in greater detail. 'I hope', he said, 'Mr. Hives and Mr. Sidgreaves may continue to watch the rise and fall of Ministers for the next twenty-five years. And if this Minister should fall shortly he will not break his heart on that account.' He agreed that the Merlin was an undoubted success but he thought that Rolls-Royce were being inhuman in not condoning the expression of hope and enthusiasm for new engines. 'The publicity that goes on about new types is inherent in the heart of man. It will be with us as long as there is hope in the land.' This was an old argument in a new guise. Beaverbrook's principal tasks were to generate enthusiasm and a sense of urgency. Hives' argument was that wishful thinking should be discouraged if it led to wishful action that ignored the warnings of experience. In another section of his report he had commented that the aircraft industry was often tempted to regard production of service machines as 'an engineering hobby instead of as a means of waging war'. Hives thought that the M.A.P. might be succumbing to this temptation where the Vulture and Sabre were concerned. 'The proverb the better is the enemy of the good, especially when the better does not exist, applies very much to the aircraft programme.' Beaverbrook replied that he did not understand the meaning of this paragraph. 'But then', he added, with a mischievous flourish, 'I have never been able to deal with temptation.'

Another serious criticism in this report referred to the confusion which existed on the subject of the Merlin-engined Wellington. The position of this aircraft had never been made clear despite the fact that its bomb-load capacity was far greater than that of the Pegasus-engined machine. In his reply to this memorandum the Minister instructed that

8. The Merlin-engined Wellington

the production of the Merlin X for the Wellington should continue and that the production of Merlin XXs should be increased though not at the expense of a decline in total output. The Vulture and the Griffon were to be brought on as swiftly as possible.

These instructions did not greatly clarify the issue. The order to increase Merlin XX production but 'not at the expense of total output' is a good example of the type of order which appears on the surface to be quite reasonable, especially to the executor, but which to the executee immediately begs a whole series of questions if it is not to be interpreted as a mere platitude.[5] During the latter part of 1940 mainly because of the changes in personnel which had taken place at both Ministries during the year, the relationship between the company and the Ministries deteriorated slightly and in consequence both sides were inclined to blame each other for the misunderstandings which arose chiefly from ineffective communication. A channel of communication which exists in theory but which is in practice closed by a conflict or lack of sympathy between individuals is not an effective channel, and there were many instances, both within the organisation of the group and between the management and the Ministries, where the paramount importance of friendly personal contact as an instrument of effective administration was made abundantly clear. The efficacy of a formal pattern of administrative organisation depends almost entirely on the informal organisation which develops within it, and which may in no way resemble it. The latter cannot be created quickly and it is easily destroyed if the turnover of personnel is too rapid. It is also more important where, as in the case of higher policy decisions, the element of mutual confidence is vital. This state of affairs is clearly revealed in comments which Hives made on the general state of engine production in the group at the end of December 1940. 'We are finding it terribly difficult in dealing with the M.A.P.', he said, 'because the whole of the staff who were responsible for the building up of our present Air Force have now disappeared and have not so far been replaced.' For this reason, as much as any other, his advocacy of the continued development of the Spitfire and Hurricane was sometimes suspected of being partisan by those who regarded all problems in terms of an irreconcilable conflict between private profit and the public interest, a bogus antithesis which has stultified many decisions.

At the end of 1940 Rolls-Royce was still committed to the production of the Vulture. Altogether 88 of these engines were produced in 1940 and 337 in 1941. It was not until March 1942 that production ceased altogether. Early in 1941 Hives had told Sir Patrick Hennessy that although Vulture engines were giving excellent service in Manchester squadrons Rolls-Royce was confident that the four-Merlined Lancaster would prove the better machine. 'We are not', he wrote, 'seeking orders for the Vulture – our anxiety is that the M.A.P. will be inviting disaster if the figures for 1942 are to be dependent on a new type of engine.' M.A.P. seemed to have no clear policy for the Vulture at this time and Lord Beaverbrook, to whom Hives had complained that a clear decision one way or the other was necessary, suggested that he would give Rolls-Royce a production order for at least 500 engines when the engine had achieved a specified performance in the Tornado airframe. Hives thought that there would be no difficulty in achieving this but he was convinced that the same production and development effort expended on the Merlin would bring far better results. In a strong memorandum to Sir Charles Craven written on 26 April he accused the M.A.P. of being more interested in producing novelties than in producing the maximum number of fighter or bomber aircraft and he suggested that the correct policy was to lay down that a given output of aircraft should be produced in a given period and that the introduction of new types should not be allowed to interfere with this. The M.A.P. was far too susceptible to foolish promises and he argued that it would be little short of criminal to change production over to new types of fighter in 1942. Again and again in 1941 Hives pressed home the argument that 'the only thing to bank on for quantity production for next year is something which exists today'. A few months earlier he had used these arguments to influence Sabre policy. Now it was the Vulture and the Whittle XII which were hypnotising the Ministry. The Sabre battle had been lost but Hives was particularly vehement in denouncing the Ministry's attempt to canvass some of Rolls-Royce's best sub-contractors to make Sabre parts. But the battle over the Vulture had been won.

The Chief of Air Staff finally concurred with this point of view on the Tornado and Typhoon and Rolls-Royce was instructed to make the maximum production effort on the high-altitude Merlin then in production and to bring on the two-stage engines then under development as fast as possible.[6] Hives also had no faith in the basic design of the Typhoon-Tornado airframe, as he had occasion to point out to Air Marshal F. J. Linnel, who was now in charge of Research and Development at the Air Ministry. The M.109F – a fully operational aircraft of the Luftwaffe – had a better all-round performance than either the Typhoon or the Tornado, both of which had been designed before the war when no one had foreseen the likelihood of the enemy operating from bases just across the Channel. In addition both aircraft were uneconomical from the production point of view. Hives estimated that at least two 109Fs could be produced with the labour and material required for the Tornado or Typhoon. He also disagreed with the contention that since the Air Staff had decided to develop the Merlin and Griffon-engined Spitfires for high-altitude work two classes of fighter should be produced to operate in specialised roles. 'My answer to this', he said, 'is that the right type will always find itself in the wrong place.' There was little doubt that the pursuit of this policy would have resulted in a much lower output of fighter aircraft in 1942.

A series of unfortunate fatal accidents on Manchester aircraft, some due to the Vulture itself, for the undeveloped state of which Rolls-Royce did not attempt to disclaim responsibility, some due to defective operation of the airscrews, finally decided Hives to insist on the abandonment of the engine. On 5 October he informed Major Bulman that Rolls-Royce was prepared, in the national interest, to scrap the Vulture V, the mark then under development, despite the fact that most of the teething troubles had just about been overcome. 'We shall set out to show that the Spitfire fitted with the latest Merlin can be very considerably improved. This also applies to other machines fitted with Merlins. This is obviously a better contribution to the national effort than spending our technical energy in proving that the Vulture is a better engine than the Sabre, because if the Tornado and Typhoon go along in parallel this is inevitably what would happen.' A desperate shortage of Merlins had developed by the end of the year despite increasing production and in view of the demands which were made on the Merlin and on Derby in the spring of 1942 it is fortunate that the M.A.P. concurred with this suggestion. A few days later Sir Charles Craven informed Derby by telephone that it had been decided to stop the production of the Vulture Tornado. Later, in 1942, when Hives was asked by Group Captain Banks whether he considered the Vulture could have been developed into an effective engine he declared that there was no doubt whatever that it could have been developed into the best engine of its class. The decision to abandon the engine was not a light-hearted one for the firm, which had spent three years developing the engine, but it was taken because the conclusion had been reached that the Vulture 'was not the engine that was required for this war'. Hives refused, in response to an invitation to do so, to criticise the Sabre, which by the end of 1942 had proved a great disappointment to its protagonists, but he concluded that had both engines been continued the result might well have been a grave national disaster. This was no exaggeration.

6 Hives Defends the Merlin

In war the operations of the enemy do not always conveniently coincide with the expectations of the strategists, and at the end of 1940 the Luftwaffe, employing 109Fs, began to operate at very great heights which the Hurricane could not reach and where even the Spitfire had very little, if any, advantage over the enemy. The Air Staff decided that the Merlin XX, which was just beginning to come forward in small numbers, should be installed in the Hurricane to improve its performance. This decision was taken because at this date Fighter Command had far more Hurricane than Spitfire Squadrons and it was considered that the all-round strength of the defence could best be maintained in this way. At a meeting at Boscombe Down on 24 December which was attended by squadron leaders from Fighter Command, the view was put forward that the R.A.F. was in danger of losing the tactical initiative to the enemy unless the ceiling of the Spitfire could be increased. The Mk. I Spitfire was being outmanoeuvred above 25,000 ft., and the Hurricane was useless above 20,000 ft. The production of the Merlin XX was still too small to re-equip both aircraft and it therefore became necessary to adopt an ingenious expedient. One of the more complex features of the Merlin XX was a low-altitude blower which made the engine more difficult to produce than previous marks. Rolls-Royce's solution to this problem was to develop a new mark of Merlin, the XLV, which had all the essential high-altitude performance features of the XX without the low-altitude blower. This engine increased the ceiling of the Spitfire by 2000 ft, and five hundred Mk. III engines were rapidly converted at Hucknall and Derby where a tremendous effort was made to complete the work with the maximum speed.[1] Another great advantage of this engine was that its installation did not require any modifications to the airframe as was the case with the Merlin XX. The Merlin XLV restored the advantage of the Spitfire at height and closed one of the gaps in the aerial defence of the island which the enemy had consistently endeavoured to discover and exploit.

The Air Staff realised that this was only a temporary expedient which could not be repeated and the company was urged to press on

9. The Vickers Supermarine Spitfire Mark VB

with the development of the Griffon as an engine for the Spitfire in 1942 and 1943. Though Hives was in general agreement with this policy he refused to allow the development of the Griffon to interfere with that of the two-stage Merlin, on which work had started early in 1940. This again was to prove a far-sighted decision. The firm stand which Hives took on the subject of developing existing engines was amply vindicated by the events of 1942 and 1943.

The last six months of 1941 saw a steady, if inadequate, rise in the output of the whole group. Both Derby and Crewe were at peak load, Glasgow was approaching full production and the output of complete engines from the Ford works in Manchester had started in August. The total production from all four factories in 1941 amounted to 12,227 engines of which 7517 were produced in the last six months of the year. The majority of these, towards the latter part of the year, were Merlin XXs which were intended to engine the Lancaster and Halifax and for the production of which both the mass-production factories (Glasgow and Fords) had been tooled up.

The production record of the firm had nevertheless come in for heavy criticism during the year. In July 1941 the Deputy Director of Engine Production, Mr Pate, wrote a report in which he severely criticised the performance of the group. He considered that the programme was in 'a complete mess' because of 'wholesale changes of type' and that the firm had shown 'the most lamentable lack of real planning ability and foresight'. Rolls-Royce, in view of the resources which had been 'made available' to them had, in his opinion, the worst record of the engine firms, and he concluded that it had 'outworn the managerial capacity of its highest control'. Mr Pate was far more concerned with the fact that the firm had not fulfilled its programmes than with its actual achievement in terms of production and development. But his criticism will not stand the test of analysis, for though from time to time the firm had virtually created a desperate shortage by producing at short notice an engine which was urgently required to increase performance in some direction or another, the total output of engines of all types was still greatly in excess of the absorption into new aircraft. Hives was well aware that he would incur criticism as a result of pursuing a strong independent policy but by this time he was convinced of its soundness. As he pointed out to the board early in 1941, if it had not been for his rigid adherence to the policy of Merlin development the only fighter machines that would have been available would have had a performance greatly inferior to that of the latest German aircraft. 'The Board should be aware that in pursuing this policy we have certainly upset some of the M.A.P. officials, but on the other hand we have added to our goodwill with the R.A.F. We had contracts to cover us to produce

10. The last wartime Spitfire Mark 21

the old type engines and as far as we were concerned it would obviously have been a very much easier manufacturing problem.' Mr Pate's criticism was obviously based on a rigid quantitative approach which ignored several of the most important factors.

One of the remedies for this state of affairs was considered to be an increase in the direct control exercised over the management. It was also considered that more effective and accurate programming would have a beneficial effect on output. But more effective programming required more complete information and both the attempt to obtain information and the attempt to apply the results of any analysis which it made possible were inclined to cause friction which at times could become serious. Ministry officials were inclined to issue requests for information without considering the effort which the provision of this information required. On 30 October Sir Alexander Dunbar wrote to Hives saying that although, as he knew, Rolls-Royce looked upon controls as a nuisance, the Light Alloy Control were unable to function effectively for lack of information on Rolls-Royce stocks. S. H. Grylls, who had to deal with requests of this kind pointed out that this would involve a week's work for the whole equipment staff and asked that the firm should be exempted from this request. 'If it is to be a precedent for similar communications', he said, 'we just have not got the staff to deal with it.' Shortly afterwards Hives himself replied that the management would do what it could to provide the information. 'I have every sympathy with controls', he added, 'and with my modest responsibility of trying to look after three factories I have acquired a very clear picture of why the League of Nations failed.'

It was deliberate M.A.P. and Air Ministry policy to interfere with the Rolls-Royce group as little as was consistent with the minimum of centralised control which the Ministries felt obliged to attempt to exercise over production as a whole. The firm's technical record was so outstanding and the dependence of the R.A.F. on Rolls-Royce engines so great that even though those in authority thought that the production record might be improved by more direct control no one was prepared to carry the responsibility for any failure which such interference might have caused. The graph which recorded the horsepower per pound of the Merlin was the thin red line of the Second World War. The management also made it quite clear that it did not regard the existing apparatus of control as being very constructive. 'We are concerned', Hives remarked in a letter to Sir Charles Craven in April 1941, 'by the number of additional officials we are getting from Government departments. We have an overseer and assistant, an R.T.O. and assistants, the A.I.D. and assistants, an M.A.P. representative and assistants. They are either sensible and acknowledge they know nothing about the problem and do nothing, or they irritate us by attempting to query decisions which they cannot possibly understand.'

The so-called production failures were in any case failures in a relative sense only – by comparison with the firm's own promises or with the even more extravagant expectations of the programme.[2] The latter were inevitably compromises, stretched between the irreducible minima of strategic requirements and the depressing maxima which a realistic appreciation of the possibilities always provided. Reasons for them could always be found and in 1941 these were not lacking. In February Hives told the board that the output of the group had definitely suffered as a result of the raids on Coventry, Birmingham and Sheffield. Crewe itself was bombed by a lone raider in the same month, resulting in both damage and casualties. This resulted in a request for additional protection from the employees. In addition as the year progressed various shortages – machine tools, labour and components (particularly carburettors) – began to occupy more and more of the management's attention. Very little could be done about machine tools.

In December 1940 S. E. Blackstone had calculated that the increased output demanded from the group would require 1175 new machine tools,[3] assuming no change in the proportion of work sub-contracted. Only 423 tools had been asked for and consequently the increased output could only be obtained by improving the machine load balancing (i.e. ensuring that the output of a line of machines was not held up by a 'bottleneck' machine), by reducing the machine hours per operation by improved methods or transferring operations from machines where these could be performed by fitters, or by increasing sub-contracting. Neither Derby nor Crewe kept accurate machine loading records at this time and consequently any general planning for the whole group was made imprecise and difficult. Blackstone considered that a reduction of machining hours from 1630 to 1250 was the most that could be hoped for under the circumstances.[4]

The limiting factor in the expansion of the Glasgow and Ford factories in particular was gear-cutting machine tools. Until July 1941 gears were produced by the batch system and on Blackstone's recommendation (which could not be carried out when it was first made because of the danger of dislocating production early in 1941) the machines were reorganised on a line system. This resulted in a remarkable improvement from 35 to 70 engine sets per week, but the programmes issued late in 1941 required an even greater increase in output. The charts from which the production build-up was controlled were the machine tool delivery charts and throughout 1941 and 1942 gear-cutting machine tools remained the limiting factor.

The Directorate of Engine Production at the M.A.P. was nevertheless critical of the achievement at Glasgow, an achievement which was much more accurately recorded statistically than that of any of the other factories. It was suggested, with some justification, that the elaboration of the reports was in inverse ratio to the output of engines. It was ironical nevertheless that the Directorate, which had a vested interest in statistics, should suggest that engines and not statistics were needed to defeat the enemy. The management would have been the first to agree that this was so but the Directorate would not readily have relinquished its right to extend the statistical stethoscope into every corner of the industrial system.

The statistics were in fact deceptive if the judgement of the Glasgow record was to be based on the output of engines only. A large volume of parts had been supplied to the other factories and for use as spares and the conversion of this output into equivalent engines revealed a production achievement which was not unimpressive. Hives challenged the Directorate to quote a better production record than Glasgow and they were unable to do so. The Glasgow output, as he was quick to point out, was achieved despite considerable interference from Ministry officials of various kinds. At times this interference had serious repercussions and on one occasion he found it necessary to give orders that under no circumstances was a certain senior official to be admitted to the Hillington factory. 'All we want to do', he wrote to Air Commodore Weedon, the Director of Repairs and Maintenance, 'is to get on with the job. If somebody is going to tell us how many spanners we require, how many stands we require, and how many cleaning tanks we require then I think it is time Rolls-Royce were relieved of any additional repairs. If you look at the map you will find that Hitler has penetrated 1,000 miles into Russia up to the present while we have been waiting for the M.A.P. to make up their minds on Vulture repairs.'

　　Rolls-Royce naturally received a high priority for labour but the shortage of skilled men, particularly of those able to hold responsible administrative positions, began to reach serious proportions in 1941. This question came up repeatedly at the Ford works in Manchester. This was the only factory making complete Merlins in England which was not managed by Rolls-Royce. Ford engineers had spent several months at Derby and maintained a close liaison, but like so many others the planning staff at Fords had underestimated the skilled labour requirements and were in consequence facing many unexpected problems in building up output. This was in no way a direct responsibility of Rolls-Royce but the Directorate of Engine Production considered that an all-round increase in production might be obtained by forming a single pool for skilled labour for all four Merlin factories. This proposal, which was put up to Hives by Major Bulman, would clearly have involved a severe drain on the skilled labour at Derby and Crewe, which had already been heavily drawn upon to help Glasgow, for the benefit of Fords. This would have restricted output of the more recent and difficult marks of Merlin, which were always in demand, and whose production inevitably required a much higher degree of skill in the initial stages. 'We shall leave you', suggested Major Bulman, 'to explore the situation by yourselves without external interference or influence, realising, however, that when you have mutually agreed as to what transfers are feasible the Ministry of Labour will be asked to exert any pressure necessary to get individuals to move.'

Hives would not countenance this proposal for a moment. He considered that the mere suggestion of such a scheme showed 'colossal impertinence' on the Directorate's part. 'You can take all the men you like away from Derby and Crewe, he replied, 'if they will go, but you also take the responsibility with them.' He considered that Fords were a much bigger organisation which was capable of looking after its own problems and that the danger of a skilled labour shortage had been quite obvious when he had visited the factory in the initial stages. The concern which this reply manifests arose partly from the fact that an excellent relationship had been established between Derby and the Manchester factory and Hives was afraid that the Ministry would upset this. He pointed out that Rolls-Royce had provided Fords with the parts for 60 complete engines to start their assembly line and he warned the Directorate that 'the day we stop providing them with pieces they will not be able to make another engine.'

The Directorate's suggestion was of course made in good faith but it showed a failure to appreciate the relative importance of production at the different factories and the great danger which would be incurred by spreading the highly-skilled technicians from Derby too thinly over the whole organisation. It also showed the somewhat theoretical approach of the administrator who, from repeated handling of the statistics of manpower, soon begins to consider that the human beings which the figures represent can be divided and multiplied and shifted from one factory or occupation to another as easily as the figures themselves. Though Major Bulman was not, as he later pointed out in reply, contemplating the transfer of more than 'a few men with actual Rolls-Royce experience' who he hoped would produce 'a snowball effect of rapid improvement', he did not realise the difficulties this involved. In a memorandum written on 7 September Hives replied at great length pointing out that he presumed Fords had been chosen because of their reserve of skilled labour at Dagenham.

On the labour position generally we came to an arrangement with the Ministry of Labour months ago that the Rolls-Royce group . . . must be judged as a whole and not as independent units. On this question of transferring labour we have had considerable experience and the men just won't go. And if they are forced to go the rest of the factory just adopts a go-slow policy. Their attitude is that the Ministry of Labour and the M.A.P. go round to the factories that are doing well and keeping up with deliveries, and that as long as you are always behind hand with the output they will not take anybody away.

Many such realities of industrial administration had not been dreamt of in the philosophies of the central planners who sought to 'co-ordinate' the output of the Rolls-Royce group from Whitehall.

Hives turned next to the question of skilled labour. As he had once before had occasion to point out, the term 'skilled' no longer meant what it had once meant in 1914. What had developed was simply a new version of the situation which was once neatly summarised by W. S. Gilbert in his immortal phrase 'when everyone is somebody then no one's anybody.' There were a number of men classed as skilled at Derby whom the management had no objection to transferring. 'But', Hives pointed out, 'they are of no use to Fords and no use to Glasgow.' The transfer problem for those who were of use was singularly acute. 'At the present time we have got the job of trying to persuade some people to go from Derby to Glasgow. The Ministry of Labour could not do it, but they will listen to my personal appeal.'

Such replies naturally did not satisfy the planners at M.A.P. for they served only to accentuate their relative helplessness in the face of the infinite plasticity of human reactions even in the most closely control-led society. The intensity, direction and location of industrial effort cannot be cast into a rigid theoretical mould without severe losses, and the complexity of the social and industrial pattern is so great that any attempt to produce adjustments which are more than marginal in character will usually defeat the objective by altering the basic rela-tionships between men and institutions in a manner which is quite unpredictable. Even the most marginal adjustments generated unforeseen difficulties and complexities.

The management had even less control of components, which were not, in many cases, the direct responsibility of Rolls-Royce, since the component firms supplied several engine manufacturers. From time to time severe shortages of certain components and accessories developed, sometimes as a result of bombing and sometimes as a result of the inability of the component manufacturers to expand production as fast as the engine factories. One of the most serious shortages in 1941 was carburettors. The S.U. Merlin carburettor was an intricate piece of mechanism which had, never before (like so many other aero-engine components) been manufactured in any quantity. Its production was also affected by bombing in 1941 and on 29 July no less than 620 engines were waiting for carburettors.

On 29 June, Hives contacted Mr Miles Thomas, managing director of the Nuffield group, and informed him that Rolls-Royce had already arranged to assist the S.U. Company by manufacturing bodies for Vulture, Peregrine, Griffon and Merlin carburettors and by making parts and jigs where necessary. He stressed that it was no use relying on Government departments to end the shortage and that only the Nuffield organisation itself could do this. On 17 July the position had become so serious that Hives offered to sacrifice engine production if necessary to help carburettor production. However the steps taken earlier in June began to have effect and within a few weeks the output recovered sufficiently to clear the accumulated engines.

Power-plants were another item that presented supply difficulties towards the end of 1941. Rolls-Royce had undertaken considerable development work on these as a result of a decision made before the war that the power-plant should be the responsibility of the engine builder rather than the airframe manufacturer. Considerable numbers were built at Hucknall and at various sub-contractors throughout the country but the output from the sub-contractors was often not sufficient to clothe the engines. Though the output of power-plants from Rolls-Royce-controlled factories was substantial the majority were produced by independent sub-contractors and by the aircraft manufacturers themselves, and the supply difficulties were mainly in this area.

Thus the years of crises completely fulfilled the predictions of the prophets even though the blitzkrieg was not quite as devastating as they had imagined it would be. Industrial production showed a remarkable resilience in the face of bombing which was fortunately not as selective as it was intensive. Once secured by the victory of the summer and autumn of 1940 the supremacy of British air power required constant reinforcement by the most intense industrial effort. The strategic momentum and tactical initiative which this effort supplied depended almost entirely on a wise distribution of resources between production and development. The maximising of this effort depended in turn on a careful assessment of the trends of enemy aircraft design and the rate of development of existing enemy types, the unexploited potentialities of existing British engines and airframes, the comparative merit of new types and the rate at which they could be safely introduced. This in its turn depended on the supply and flexibility of certain specialised factors of production such as machine tools and the most highly skilled labour.

The decision process was thus exceedingly complex, even though the ultimate objective was so clear and unequivocal. War may well simplify the economic problem but if the above must be considered a 'simple' situation its ramifications in time of peace should not be underrated. No hard and fast rules could be laid down but the apparatus of measurement and control was improved and by the end of 1941 the relationship between output and the various variables by which resources were measured were more clearly ascertainable. It became possible in consequence to reduce the arbitrary element in the prediction of quantities and to assess the limits of expansion of the existing capacity. It was yet some time however before Ministers and officials began to show an implicit understanding of the significance of the programme in its three-fold function as a psychological, a statistical and an administrative instrument. Even at the end of the war this tri-functional character had not been fully appreciated but in the following three years the general interdependence of these functions became much better understood. The M.A.P. and the Air Ministry began to realise that though programmes would not perform miracles, miracles might on occasion be performed without programmes. The technique was an imperfect if essential method of illuminating and guiding the flow of industrial production. The trend towards 'realism' in the later years of the war is an indication of the fact that the Ministries found it both easier and more useful to adapt programmes to reality than reality to programmes.

Within this complex framework the policy of Rolls-Royce did not greatly change. The integrity and soundness of Hives' judgement and the tenacity with which he fought the case for Merlin development ensured that the R.A.F. did not lack the right aircraft in 1941 or 1942 and earned him a considerable and well-deserved reputation. Despite criticism which was largely, if not always, ill-founded, he managed to maintain the full independence of the management during a most crucial period when many who were inevitably somewhat remote from reality, if not lacking in authority, must have been tempted by the urgency of the situation to interfere. On the whole the mutual confidence between the Directorates and the management was enhanced by the interchange of frank and forthright criticism which often reflected the passion of deeply-held convictions and the concern of men who knew that a mistake could at best cost many lives and at worst lose the war. By comparison the last three years from 1942 to 1945 seem a period of calm in which a task was completed on the basis of foundations well and truly laid in the strenuous and exacting years which culminated in the Battle of Britain and its immediate aftermath.

7 The 'Meteor' Tank-engine Project

After the fall of France it became public knowledge that the British Army did not possess a tank which was equal in performance or firepower to the tanks of the German Panzer divisions. British tanks were notoriously underpowered and underarmed and most of these were lost in France. This deplorable state of affairs was due to a variety of causes. The funds allotted for tank development work in the twenties and thirties – which the War Office made no great efforts to increase – were negligible, during rearmament the claims of the Air Force were so great that the Army was perforce neglected, few large firms apart from Vickers-Armstrong found it profitable to develop and produce tanks, and both the General Staff and the regiments of the line had little interest in tanks and armoured vehicles generally. The role which armoured divisions would play in the land battles of the Second World War had not been envisaged, except by a few eccentric officers such as Captain Liddell Hart and Colonel Martel.

There was in consequence no shadow tank industry, and, because of the inadequacy of the funds allotted, even those firms which would in the normal course of events have acted as technical parents to other suitable firms found that their resources in personnel and technical knowledge were totally inadequate. In the aircraft industry the main development work had been done, the structure of a flexible production organisation established, and though highly skilled technicians were always in short supply there was a sufficient number to carry the load of continued expansion and development. In the tank and tank-engine industry this was not the case. The development work had been confined largely to the tank hull and suspension and to adapting, for use in tanks, engines which were either obsolete – as in the case of the Liberty – or unsuitable because of their lack of power. Underpowered commercial engines designed for other purposes were installed in various combinations whose reliability was small compensation for the absurdly inadequate performance which they provided.

During 1939 and 1940 very little could be done about this and tank production had to be planned on the basis of the existing machines and engines. The emphasis in the first few months of the war, especially after the fall of France, was on quantity at all costs, and, though some thought was given to the development of higher-powered engines, little was achieved because of the hopeless inadequacy of the existing resources for tank development.

The management of Rolls-Royce had never expected to be involved in the production and development of tank-engines, nor did it have any particular desire to do so in 1940. Though Rolls-Royce engines had been fitted in armoured cars for many years the firm had never been asked to consider designing or adapting engines for tanks. Had such an approach been made after 1935 both the firm and the Air Ministry would probably have disapproved of the idea. In 1940 however Mr W. A. Robotham, whose chassis design and development division at Belper was not in general adaptable to work on aero-engines, realised that his staff could be much more usefully employed working on specific projects where their specialised knowledge would be valuable than if they were disbanded. He also knew about the serious tank-engine situation and decided on his own initiative to give some attention to the problem in October 1940. He thereupon contacted H. Spurrier, jun., a director of the Leyland Company, and investigated the whole tank position with him.

The Leyland Company was at this time manufacturing a tank with which they were thoroughly dissatisfied, having had little to do with its design, and Spurrier was certain that Rolls-Royce could provide considerable assistance on power-plant development. Early in November Robotham visited the tank testing ground at Farnborough and examined the tanks then undergoing trial. His report was most unfavourable. Technical development, which had been in the hands of 'one or two railway companies directed by a Board consisting of civil servants and military advisers' was hopelessly out of touch with advances which had been made elsewhere in the engineering industry. There was very little standardisation and production had been so slow that the Mechanisation Board at the War Office were forced to allow commercial vehicle manufacturers to have some say in tank design and development.

The Leyland Company had been asked to go into production on the Mk. VI Liberty-engined tank and both Robotham and Spurrier considered that this would be a most retrograde step. The immediate alternative was to convert a standard Rolls-Royce engine into a tank-engine and Robotham decided to investigate forthwith the possibility of adapting the Kestrel, a naturally aspirated engine for which the Air Force demand was not nearly as great as it was for the Merlin. Bench tests proved that this engine occupied less space and gave considerably more power than the Liberty but the engine did not provide the 20 h.p. per ton ratio which was considered to be the minimum standard towards which it was desirable to work. The next engine to be considered was the Merlin. This was a supercharged engine requiring some adaptation but this was not difficult to carry out and a modified version suitable for installation in the Mk. VI tank in place of the Liberty was rapidly produced. This was the engine which became known as the Meteor.

It was essential that the replacement of the Liberty should be able to fit into the engine compartment of the tanks then in production for the Liberty engine and it so happened that the displacement of the Merlin was exactly the same as that of the Liberty, though its bore and stroke were different, making it a more compact engine. It was obvious at the outset that a great deal of development work would have to be done on the Meteor to make it a suitable engine for tank work. It was equally clear that if the British tank programme was to be dependent on the Liberty – an engine designed in 1917 which, even by 1941, had been developed up to a maximum power output of 340 h.p. – British armour would not be able to stand up to a Panzer division. A surprisingly large number of responsible people scattered throughout the military and civilian tank hierarchies seemed quite incapable of appreciating the fact and supported their attitude with the most ingenious and convincing rationalisations. In some cases these rationalisations were so strongly entrenched that it is unlikely that even personal experience of the fire from German 75 mm guns in the desert in 1941 – without being able to reply – would have served to convince the diehards that existing British tanks were virtually a tactical liability.

As soon as the original specifications of the Meteor[1] had been established Robotham realised that the steering, track, hull and cooling system would also have to be modified. In view of the fact that Rolls-Royce was also working on the 40 mm automatic gun for the Navy he advocated that his staff should investigate the development of the turret 'with a view to improving its hitting power and versatility'. In his report to Hives on these developments Robotham put forward the opinion that it 'would be little short of a crime for Liberty engines to be produced rather than Meteors because of lack of energy on our part', and added that he hoped to have a Meteor running in a tank by the end of March 1941.

Hives concurred fully with Robotham's point of view. In a report to the board he mentioned that Rolls-Royce had received a request for help from Leylands and that Robotham had been studying the problem. 'The conclusions we have arrived at are that the position as regards the power plant for tanks is just terrible – we cannot imagine anything worse. There is no such thing as a decent tank engine. The best one they have is the Liberty engine designed in the U.S.A. in 1915–16 which has been botched up or modified to go into a tank. The gearbox and transmission is, if possible, in an even worse state than the engine. We find the Midland Railway designing gearboxes on methods which were discarded twenty years ago.' Hives told the board that on the production side Rolls-Royce could do nothing but that they would give all the technical assistance which they could. He informed Lord Beaverbrook on 18 December that draughtsmen had arrived from Leylands to work on the Merlin and on a gearbox. 'Our picture of the tank position', he said, 'is that they are desperately in need of help.'

Intensive development work began on the Meteor to adapt it for installation in the existing Mk. VI hull and at the end of March a meeting to discuss progress was held at the Directorate of Tank Design. This was most discouraging and Robotham came away under the impression that it had been decided not to produce the engine. It seemed to him that every conceivable objection had been raised and that most of them were invalid. On the following day he addressed a strong memorandum to the Director of Tank Design (at this time Mr J. Weir) in an endeavour to persuade him to reverse this decision. He pointed out that Rolls-Royce had no financial interest whatsoever in the Meteor, and that the mere fact that it had been named the Leyland Meteor should have been sufficient evidence of this. The engine was due to undergo its first tests in a tank within a week and Robotham thought it quite absurd that a decision should be taken not to produce the engine before any attempt had been made to discover whatever advantages it possessed in the way of durability and performance. The reasons given at this meeting why the Meteor should not be produced were the following:

(1) It was impossible for 'manufacturing considerations' to justify putting a new tank-engine into production.

(2) It was impossible to use the additional horsepower of the Meteor because of track limitations. Even if it were possible the increased performance *would not be of interest* to the General Staff.
(3) What was really required was a new design of oil engine.
(4) The General Staff thought that the design of infantry and cruiser tanks should remain separate. They did not want a fast infantry tank or a heavily armoured cruising tank.
(5) The Directorate was more interested in the work which Rolls-Royce was doing on transmission and steering.

Not one of these arguments was of any substance. The first was contradicted by the fact that Leylands stated that they could produce the Meteor as quickly as the Liberty. The second argument was absurd. If the speed of the tank was kept constant the increased engine output could be converted to armour and the ground pressure (the main determinant of track life) kept constant by increasing the track width. The additional horsepower offered a choice between armour and speed. Robotham could not credit the argument that the General Staff was not interested in increased performance. As for the argument that an oil engine was required, he pointed out that Italian tanks with oil engines had burnt very easily and that in any case the oil engine had the threefold disadvantage of greater weight and bulk per horsepower and of requiring more man-hours to produce. In addition tank commanders in the field realised at an early stage of the war that the relative dangers of fire due to oil and petrol engines were quite overshadowed by the risk of cordite fires caused by inadequately stowed ammunition in the fighting compartment.

The fourth argument was incomprehensible. No tank, Robotham pointed out, need go faster than its driver wished it to go and there was no armoured fighting vehicle which did not require better protection if this could be obtained without any sacrifice in performance. Finally, the advantage to be gained by studying the gearbox and transmission alone was very much less than the immense improvement in performance which would be obtained from using a high-powered engine. 'You will see from the above observations', he concluded, 'that our discussion with you in London, far from giving us a clear picture as to where our technical ability can be of most service to the country, has left us with the impression that we can be of no service whatever since we are incapable of understanding the fundamental requirements of tracked fighting vehicles.' He suggested that in the national interest the Leyland Meteor should be given a fair trial and the production decision

11. The Rolls-Royce Meteor tank engine

postponed until after the tests had been carried out. The Director of
Tank Development replied that he was substantially in agreement with
these arguments and that he and his staff had merely been putting the
contrary point of view at the meeting.

The initial trials of the Mk. VI tank with the Meteor took place the
following week but, as Robotham was quick to notice, no military
spectators and not a single member of the Tank Board were present.
This was not exactly encouraging. The trials proved, nevertheless, that
the Meteor gave the tank a comfortable margin though this was
dependent, with the existing transmission, on a very skilful gear-
change. The existing gearbox and clutch made any sort of change 'a
matter of superlative judgement and superhuman strength'.

On 27 April Robotham reported that he had received a verbal
intimation that the Meteor was to be in production within ten months
and that the production target was to be from 150 to 200 engines a

month by the spring of 1942. There were, however, a good many difficulties to be overcome. Many of these were a legacy of peace, the manifestation in another guise of the problem which had occupied Robotham and his staff for several years before the war.

> We have had meetings with various people at the D.T.D. and also with Generals Pope and Burrows. We find the army very open-minded but they do not seem to understand the production difficulties involved by some of their requirements. . . . We are sure that tank pieces have got to be rationalised for the best results to be achieved from the overloaded British production facilities. . . . There can be no justification for four completely different types of engine for heavy tanks, and also several types of steering, transmission, tracks and cooling.

On 26 May it was decided to produce six prototype battle-cruiser tanks of a type which Robotham had suggested four months previously. All six were to be engined by the Meteor. Three prototypes were to be built by Leylands and three by the Nuffield group. On 16 May 1941 Leylands were given a firm contract for 1200 Meteor engines. Their design specification was by no means simple. The engine had to be suitable for two hulls – the Mk. VI and Mk. VII tanks, two cooling systems – Nuffied and Rolls-Royce, three transmissions – Nuffield, Rolls-Royce and Merritt-Brown, and had to be installationally interchangeable with the Liberty.

Unfortunately this determination to go ahead with the Meteor did not last. At a Ministry of Supply meeting in Birmingham on 30 May, at which the industry was widely represented, the choice of an engine for the heavier type of cruiser tank was again exhaustively discussed. It was claimed from some sides that the Meteor had not proved itself as a tank-engine. Mr Miles Thomas, referring to the Liberty, said that 'age is not necessarily a criterion of ability', where engines were concerned and advocated the production of the Liberty rather than the Meteor. Hives again emphasised the fact that Rolls-Royce was too heavily committed on aero-engines to be able to promise more than advice and technical assistance. It was nevertheless agreed that Leylands would proceed with tooling for the Meteor which they now expected to have in production by February 1942.

During the following three weeks it became increasingly obvious to all concerned that the Leyland Company had done nothing to implement this decision and on 21 June Robotham informed Hives that

12. W. A. Robotham

Leylands' enthusiasm for the Meteor project seemed to be waning. He attributed this to several factors. One of the most important was that the M.A.P. would not, at this stage, agree to the Rolls-Royce group supplying Leylands with unbalanced production pieces. He also believed that an investigation of the Meteor drawings had 'frightened their works' and that for this reason the company had returned to advocating a 350 h.p. oil engine of their own design. Several other factors, some connected with the Meteor itself, also contributed to this reversal of policy. When fitted in the Mk VI tank the Meteor proved to be 30 per cent less efficiently cooled than the Liberty, employing the highly inefficient cooling system of the latter engine. The Meteor, giving some 75 per cent more power than the Liberty, was used in the same size compartment despite the 20 per cent increase in fuel tankage and the provision of enclosed air cleaners. At the Birmingham meeting, Hives had given the Leyland officials the impression that Rolls-Royce could not be held responsible for the Meteor installation, an announcement which had disturbed some of the Leyland engineers. The meeting has also been warned that the aluminium head of the Meteor might cause trouble. In addition, the production man-hour figures had proved somewhat alarming to Leylands and Robotham admitted that these were 'somewhat disconcerting if presented in their blackest form to the uninitiated'. In consequence, Leylands now endeavoured to enlist Robotham's support for their own engine, which was itself still in an experimental stage. They believed that both the Meteor and their own diesel could be developed in parallel.

Robotham was not persuaded. He pointed out that the Leyland diesel engine had been discussed in December 1940 and turned down on that occasion because it was inferior to the Meteor. He refused to go back on this position unless Leylands could convince him in a written report that such a step was in the national interest. Leylands agreed to produce such a report but Robotham did not find it convincing. He considered that his staff had done very valuable work in designing a tank-engine which would fulfil general staff requirements and concluded that 'it would be a crime if this contribution to the war effort were to be wasted'.

On 21 June 1941 Sidgreaves summarised the position in a letter to Sir Charles Craven at the M.A.P. He pointed out that Leylands had received an order for 1200 Meteors two months previously and that instead of accepting this responsibility the firm was endeavouring to persuade the Ministry of Supply officials to go back on their previous decision and produce the Leyland diesel.'The position at the present time', he continued, 'is that the Ministry of Supply are still convinced of the urgent necessity for the supply of Meteor engines. Leylands have backed out and do not wish to take the responsibility for these engines but would be willing, if instructed, to act as sub-contractors. We have made it clear to everybody that Rolls-Royce have no desire to produce engines for tanks but we have an intense desire to provide the maximum effort to win the war.' Sidgreaves considered that it was of vital importance that the project should continue. There was no doubt whatever that a higher-powered engine was urgently required in British tanks and the Meteor had the advantage of being able to employ Merlin scrap and to benefit from Merlin production when this was out of balance. He concluded by emphasising that if Rolls-Royce were to undertake any production responsibility this would have to be arranged through the shadow factory at Hillington.

On the following day, Hives received a letter from the managing director of Leylands, Mr Liardet, in which the latter stated that he thought it best that Rolls-Royce should continue independently in order to avoid 'wasteful friction'. He offered to provide sub-contract assistance and enclosed a copy of a letter to Mr W. E. Rootes, Chairman of the Supply Council, informing the latter of the Leyland Company's decision to continue with the development of their own engine. 'We felt strongly', he concluded, 'that to set up a plant separate to and duplicate of the Rolls-Royce for the production of this engine was basically wrong.'

On 23 June Robotham received a letter from Spurrier in which the latter mentioned that the Minister of Supply (now Lord Beaverbrook) had visited Leylands and had given his approval to a scheme to produce three prototype Mk. VII tanks having a Meteor, a Leyland and a Liberty engine. While these prototypes were being built Leylands were to make a careful survey of the production requirements 'having in mind the probable necessity of manufacturing one or possibly both types in large quantities and spread over the more important commercial type engine manufacturers'. Spurrier pointed out that the reasons for this decision were the refusal of the M.A.P. to sanction the supply of parts from Rolls-Royce and the fact that Leylands had been told that they could not expect the machine tools which would enable them to produce the complete engine independently of Rolls-Royce. He also stressed the point that a study of man-hour requirements carried out by Mr Grimshaw of Leylands and Mr D. R. Abbot Anderson of Rolls-Royce had shown that the Meteor required 2500 man-hours (of which 1200 were machining hours) compared with a total of 800 for the diesel.

Spurrier visualised three alternatives. The Leyland could be placed in production as soon as possible followed by the Meteor on a national basis when capacity became available, or the Meteor could be put into production immediately and the diesel dropped completely, or vice versa. 'I am mindful', he concluded, 'of the fact that Leylands hold a Ministry order for 1,200 Meteor engines. This nevertheless cannot in any way assist our present problems and we shall be obliged to hold up the placing of material orders against this until settlement has been reached. You must believe me when I tell you that these recent steps taken by us have in no way been influenced by any anxiety on our part to put an engine of our design before one of yours or of anyone else's for that matter.' The Leyland management was clearly adopting a very cautious attitude. They were not prepared to take the risk of throwing the full weight of their organisation behind the Meteor and preferred to spread the risk, and dissipate their efforts, by developing and producing three engines simultaneously. This attitude indicated that Leylands could also be accused of subservience to the long-established tradition of multiplicity in the British internal combustion engine industry.

Since the lack of drive and enthusiasm behind their Meteor order could not be attributed to any serious disadvantage of the Meteor[2] or to production difficulties which could not be solved, given the will to do so, Robotham had no alternative but to conclude that the Leyland Company preferred the easier solution of producing its own engine, irrespective of any question of commercial advantage. This was naturally substantial, since had the Leyland engine been adopted in the majority of British tanks this would have put the company in a strong position for future orders. Robotham replied to Spurrier that he could see no advantage whatever to be gained from putting another 12-cylinder 350 h.p. tank-engine into production when both the Liberty and the Vauxhall engine of this power were already in production.

A meeting at the Directorate of Tank Design took place on 27 June to discuss this question. Robotham was strongly opposed to the proposal that the two engines should be produced in parallel and he argued that it was essential to develop a higher-powered engine as soon as possible. The British Army already had too many low-powered, under-armed and under-armoured tanks and Robotham appreciated only too clearly that it was a question either of overcoming the conservatism of the British manufacturers, and the policies towards which they were predisposed by the structure of the industry, or of sacrificing mobility and firepower in British armoured divisions. J. Weir, the Director of Tank Development, endeavoured to balance the opposing views by pointing out that the Leyland diesel engine was considered by them to be a solution to their production difficulties. That this point should have been raised is interesting in that it indicates the quite extraordinary confusion of objectives which must have existed at this time. The objective of producing the maximum number of the best tanks was presumably to have been overriden by the objective of producing a tank-engine which particular factories would have found it easy to produce. The Leyland engineers endeavoured to suppport their case by strong criticism of the cooling problems on the Meteor, which had not yet been completely solved although intensive work was being carried out on them at the tank division in Belper. The question of the M.A.P. decision was raised but it was agreed that, given sufficient pressure and authority, this decision was not irrevocable. Mr Weir supported Robotham in pointing out that there had been no material changes in the relative position of the various tank engines since the decision in favour of the Meteor had been made, but Leylands were apparently not prepared to act on this decision.

This trend of events exasperated Robotham, who had no commercial or personal axes to grind (since the financial interests of his company were in no way involved) and who realised more clearly than most what a disaster the continued production of under-powered tanks might cause. On 4 July he complained in a letter to the Director of Tank Development that he had 'become involved in a nightmare'. He had, he pointed out, to spend most of his time 'defending a simplified version of the engine that won the Battle of Britain from the following accusations:

1. That it cannot be made
2. That if it could be made it cannot be cooled
3. That in any case the people who are installing it are so incompetent that its performance in a track vehicle will be no better than that of a partly developed oil engine . . . two thirds its size.

Three Meteor engines had actually been built by this time and Robotham pointed out that a great deal of work had been carried out to satisfy the requirement that the Meteor should be interchangeable with the Liberty.

It was becoming abundantly clear to all concerned that there was little hope of the Leyland management taking energetic action to produce the Meteor in their factories. It was not difficult for them to find excuses for not doing so and to oppose the project on technical and production grounds. No engineering project of this magnitude is exempt from technical difficulties and uncertainties. Leyland's two main excuses were that the M.A.P. would not release parts and that the cooling system had not proved satisfactory. On 12 July Spurrier informed Robotham that he had 'grave doubts' as to whether or not the new cooling system could 'ever be made to produce results in its existing form'. On 17 July Robotham informed Hives that Leylands had called a special meeting at the Directorate, to which he had not been invited, to stress the hopelessness of the cooling problem. This complaint was in fact poorly founded,[3] although it was no doubt based on the sincere convictions of the Leyland engineers. But whatever the reasons for their behaviour, there was no doubt by this time that the Leyland Company did not intend to manufacture the Meteor.[4] Hives informed Lord Beaverbrook and Sir Charles Craven that he was thoroughly dissatisfied with the progress that was being made and suggested that it was high time someone took steps to remedy the situation. On 21 July Sidgreaves suggested in a letter to the Chairman of the Supply Council, W. E. Rootes, that the Ministry of Supply should order its engines through the Ministry of Aircraft Production. It was evident by this time that if any engines at all were to be produced Rolls-Royce would have to take responsibility for their production as well as for their development.

On 23 July Robotham discussed the situation with General Crawford, then Deputy Director-General of Tank Supply. Crawford thought that Leylands would be unable to keep their promises and he recommended that Rolls-Royce should not rely on Leylands' ability to produce the parts which were special to the Meteor. He suggested that the firm should contact the Meadows Company, which had a factory with 120 machine tools immediately available. This company was producing its own flat twelve engine for the tank programme and was interested in the idea of producing the Meteor. Robotham agreed to visit this factory and in the meantime at a Ministry of Supply Conference on 29 July it was decided to cancel the order to Leylands and to order the 1200 engines through the M.A.P. Leylands were asked to wind up their work on the project and to concentrate on their own engine. The Meteor development work was to be continued by Rolls-Royce, who had in any case done nearly all of it and who now became fully responsible for production as well. Both Hives and the M.A.P. had foreseen this development, which they had wished to avoid, but it was imperative that the work should be carried out by some responsible firm and it seemed unlikely that this would be done unless the impetus came from Derby. The M.A.P. finally agreed to release surplus parts under certain limited circumstances but it was necessary, if any production was to be achieved, to find a separate factory for the manufacture of the special parts and the final assembly of the engine.

Robotham visited the Meadows factory with General Crawford on 30 July. This small factory employed 2000 men and produced specialist engines. It manufactured no less than 40 different types of engine and had an output of 100 per month. Robotham was favourably impressed by the organisation and formed the opinion that Meadows would be able, with suitable assistance, to assemble and test 160 engines a month by May 1942, though this would depend on the provision of the necessary pieces by Rolls-Royce. Eighty-five per cent of the Meteor parts were common to the Meteor and Merlin and it was decided that Meadows and Austins together would manufacture the special pieces. The Meadows factory was to arrange facilities for assembly and testing at the rate of 200 engines a month. The first deliveries were requested for February 1942. It was estimated that on a basis of 1300–1500 machining hours per Meteor a total of 600 machine tools would be required if these worked a 100-hour week.

The Directorate itself now began to take a more optimistic view of the possibilities and on 4 August G. C. Usher (then Director-General of Tank Supply) informed Sidgreaves that the Army would require all the engines which Rolls-Royce could possibly produce if the Meteor proved to be the success which was anticipated. Sidgreaves replied that a special development section had been set up at Belper to centralise control of development and that Rolls-Royce was not waiting for written contract authority to go ahead.

Several matters relevant to the Meteor were discussed at a Ministry of Supply meeting on 16 August which was attended by Major Bulman representing the Ministry of Aircraft Production. A number of difficulties were raised, especially by Major Bulman, who pointed out that it would be dangerous for the Meadows factory to plan its production on the assumption that the Rolls-Royce aero lines would always be unbalanced and therefore producing parts surplus to aero-engine requirements. The Ministry of Labour representative was disturbed by the prospect of the Meadows Company erecting a new factory near their Wolverhampton plant but Mr Hamill, the managing director, pointed out that they would not require more than a thousand men. It was agreed that the instructions to proceed should be issued and that, until the Meadows organisation was ready, Rolls-Royce should allocate all machine tools received on the Meteor scheme to their existing sub-contractors. The Meadows Company was to act as a sub-contractor to Rolls-Royce but was to have direct control over the expansion of its own factory. This seemed a sensible and workmanlike arrangement and it was decided that Rolls-Royce should prepare a brochure setting out their expansion proposals in full. This was done immediately.

The brochure emphasised that the company had undertaken this project solely in the national interest and that it would derive no fee or profit whatever. It demanded that the management should have a completely free hand in the allocation of machine tools throughout the group on the basis that Rolls-Royce factories would supply Meadows with parts equivalent in machine-tool hours to the number of tools which had been absorbed by Rolls-Royce. The brochure stressed the fact that the management had only undertaken the 'preliminary' responsibility for the 'preliminary' supply of these engines and that the M.A.P. had been given an assurance that the production of Meteors would under no circumstances be allowed to interfere with the production of aero-engines or spares. Three phases of operation were contemplated. The first phase covered the supply of 1000 engines in two batches of 500 (the order having been reduced by 200), the second phase covered the creation of capacity for the production of 50 engines a week and the third phase covered the creation of capacity for a production of a much larger output of engines. General Crawford had suggested in July that the eventual output might be as high as 700 engines a month. Four sources of production were to be employed. The output of aero machine lines was to be supplemented by the provision of balancing plants. New sub-contractors were to be brought in and cast iron and other lower-grade materials would be employed if necessary. Parts which were rejected by A.I.D. were to be employed for the Meteor provided that they were suitable and as many parts as possible were to be bought out. Commercial quality studs, nuts and bolts were considered to be suitable. A block grant of £1 million to finance the project was requested.

On 12 September Lord Beaverbrook, who was impressed by the brochure, telegraphed Derby as follows:

The British Government has given you an open credit of one million pounds. This is a certificate of character and reputation without precedent or equal.

At a Ministry of Supply meeting on 15 September, I. Spens, the Director of Contracts, accepted the brochure as it stood though he believed that the M.A.P. were not enthusiastic about this expansion of Rolls-Royce's responsibilities. In view of the state of aero-engine supply at this time this reluctance was not surprising, but it was natural that the Ministry of Supply officials should wish to guarantee as far as possible that their own output would not suffer in consequence. The intention of Rolls-Royce was quite clear from the brochure. The company intended to throw its weight behind the project for an interim period to get production securely established, to build up the technical development organisation at Belper, to educate an assembly firm up to the point where it could accept full responsibility for production and to do all this without in any way affecting the aero-engine effort.

As soon as Rolls-Royce had accepted this interim responsibility, however, the Ministry began to increase its orders. On 26 September J. D. Crozier, the Director of Tank Supplies, informed Hives that 1900 engines would be required to meet the tank programme in 1942, followed by a further 2100 by June 1943. He suggested that the 1942 programme could be met by a production of fity engines per week if this began in March. This was clearly beyond the capacity of the organisation or the intention of the management. On 5 October Hives defined Rolls-Royce's plan in a letter to G. C. Usher, the Director-General. It was proposed to build at Belper, from sub-standard Merlin parts, 25 prototype Meteors which it was expected would be completed in three or four months. In the meantime Meadows would be instructed to produce 500 sets of the special Meteor parts.

The Ministry soon realised that Rolls-Royce could not possibly be expected to carry the responsibility for a full-scale production programme for tank engines. The demand for 1900 engines in 1942 had been made without any reference to the production facilities available and at a Ministry of Supply meeting on 15 October the possibility of expanding the production facilities was explored. The Meteor, whose success was now beyond any doubt, had been chosen as the primary power plant for the Mk. VII tank which was scheduled to come into full production in 1943. Four thousand of these tanks were called for during that year. Robotham, who attended this meeting, pointed out that in terms of total horsepower required the figure for the first quarter of 1943 (1,369,000 h.p.) represented a 300 per cent increase on the figure for the last quarter of 1941 (452,000 h.p.). He suggested that this could only be obtained from new tools, new plant, better utilisation of existing capacity or from production in the United States. It was quite obvious that it would be foolish to rely on Meteor production to supply this demand and Leylands advocated that the gap should be filled by production of their diesel. The alternative was the Liberty. Mr Oliver Lucas, a member of the Tank Board, was against the proposal to manufacture the Leyland on the familiar grounds that there were two engines of this size already in production, that the new tanks required 600 h.p. and that since the Leyland engine had two superchargers and two injection pumps it could not claim to be a simple engine to produce. It also had a higher ratio of power to volumetric capacity than the Liberty and was more prone to teething troubles. It was therefore decided to allocate the whole Leyland plant to the Liberty, the Meadows plant to the Meteor, and to explore the possibility of expanding production in the United States.

Robotham returned from this meeting satisfied that the Chairman of the Tank Board intended to do all in his power to see that the Meteor was allocated a fair share of the available manufacturing facilities but he regretted the decision to allocate any manufacturing facilities to the Liberty unless it could be shown that the Meteor was twice as difficult to produce.

By the end of October 1941 six engines were in existence and the final production installation was on test in a mock-up hull of the new type of tank which had been evolved round the Meteor and for whose design the organisation at Belper was very largely responsible. Technical progress during the year had been substantial[6] but production seemed as far off as ever. At a Meteor production meeting at Belper on 27 October it was pointed out that Meadows had just received a further order for 1000 of their own engines and that it therefore was unlikely that they would be able to devote any of their existing plant to Meteor production. It was decided that nevertheless the production order for 500 special parts should be placed.

Development work continued meanwhile at Belper though Robotham was severely handicapped by a shortage of draughtsmen and detailers. The production specification of the first 1000 engines had been stabilised and on the basis of the experience already acquired

Robotham proposed that several modifications be introduced on the next mark of the engine. The most important of these was the use of a cast-iron cyclinder block. The weight consideration was of negligible importance in a tank and this change would have the great advantage of reducing the dependence of the Meteor on the output of the light-alloy foundries whose capacity was already severely strained by the demands of aero-engine production. Robotham considered that the installation was too complicated, inaccessible and expensive in man-hours from the maintenance point of view and he proposed several modifications to meet these criticisms. He expected that the development work required would be completed by the end of 1942.

The production situation showed no signs of improving in November and December. At a Rolls-Royce production meeting on 11 November Hives pointed out that Meadows had not been relieved of further production orders for their own products and that it seemed unlikely that they would be able to provide any more assistance than Leylands in getting the Meteor into production. The Birmingham Railway Carriage and Wagon Company, which was producing the Mk. VII hull for the Meteor, had also been asked to 'parent' a tank fitted with the Liberty. Work was also proceeding on a Mk. VIII designed to take either the Liberty or the Meteor. Robotham thought that this would result in a dissipation of effort in all directions and he warned the Directorate that its development should not be hurried at the expense of the other tank. 'I think that eventually we will convince them', he remarked in his progress report, 'that they have enough models of unreliable tanks to last them until the end of the war.'

Hives indicated his growing dissatisfaction with the progress being made on the production side at the Meadows factory in a memorandum sent to Lord Beaverbrook on 12 December. This was prompted by two factors. The first of these was that details of the heavy bomber programme had just been received and it was quite obvious that the increase in output from the Rolls-Royce group which this required would demand a tremendous effort. On the Meteor side it was also apparent that unless capacity was made available for assembly and test in an existing factory, or a completely new factory built – which would have had to be completely controlled by Rolls-Royce – there was little chance of the production of Meteors starting in 1942. He therefore recommended that the entire tank engine position should be reviewed.

On the development side of the Meteor tank engine we have

maintained our promises and shall continue to do so and I am satisfied that we are making a real contribution to the engineering side of tanks. We still hold the view that the Meteor engine as a project cannot be neglected if better tanks are required. Except for your generous gesture of the allocation of £1 million we have received no help from the Ministry of Supply as regards the production of Meteor engines. The impression we get is that the Meteor is looked upon as a sideline. In the case of Henry Meadows . . . when we press them to manufacture more of the pieces they remind us that they are still committed to a big programme of other types of engines.

In conclusion Hives suggested that the best way out of the impasse was to review the entire contract arrangements and make the Meadows organisation entirely responsible for the Meteor.

Lord Beaverbrook left for the United States shortly after this and the matter was naturally referred to the Director-General of Tank Supply for his comment. G. C. Usher's reply revealed the confusion which existed at the Ministry.

My understanding is that the development to final design stage of the Meteor engine is entirely in the hands of Rolls-Royce who have been given all the facilities which they requested and were given an authorisation of £1 million to provide for the additional capacity which they considered would be necessary for the production of these engines. . . . Hives' letter to the Minister gives me the impression that he is doubtful whether he can produce what he originally promised and is now attempting to hedge and throw responsibility on the Ministry before fully discussing his difficulties with us. . . . I am not aware of any technical development work on tank engines which is interfering with Meadows giving the whole of their technical attention to the development of the Meteor engine. . . . It appears that the immediate problem is to finalise the contract position as affecting Rolls-Royce, Meadows, the M.A.P. and the Ministry of Supply. The essential point is to decide whether this contract is to be placed with Henry Meadows direct, with a contract to Rolls-Royce for technical supervision and supply of design details only.

This reply reveals that the Directorate had not understood the nature of the proposal which Rolls-Royce had made in the original brochure. From the beginning Rolls-Royce had considered it necessary to retain technical parentage and carry out technical development, for which the organisation at Belper had been developed and expanded. No other company was in a position to do this. It was equally obvious that no other company under the control of the Ministry of Supply considered itself competent to produce the entire Meteor engine. In view of this situation Rolls-Royce had obtained the sanction of the M.A.P. to employ machine tools allocated by the Ministry of Supply for Meteor production to increase the output of the Rolls-Royce group sufficiently to balance the supply of those Merlin parts which were suitable for Meteor production. A balanced allocation of machine tools within the Rolls-Royce group would in any case have achieved a far greater total increase in output than their employment in a separate factory. Rolls-Royce could not undertake to produce the special Meteor components since this was obviously inconsistent with the promise to the M.A.P. that Meteor production would under no circumstances absorb effort that should be devoted to aero-engines. It was thus essential that a separate organisation should manufacture the special pieces in the required quantities and assemble and test the engines. The Meadows Company had agreed to do this but had shown little sign of fulfilling their obligation by the end of 1941.

The true position was set out very forcibly in a memorandum which Hives produced in reply to the allegation that Rolls-Royce were seeking to evade responsibility and to shift this on the Ministry of Supply.

We wish to correct any impression that Rolls-Royce are not going to keep their promise as regards the delivery of 500 Meteor engines in 1942. The 500 engines will be supplied. Our real anxiety is for 1943 onwards.

The difficulty the country finds itself in in the production of satisfactory tanks can be attributed to the fact that previous to the war there was no tank industry and therefore there was no firm basis and engineering staff to expand from. The very fact that the tank engine which the Ministry of Supply has decided to produce in large quantities is based on the Liberty engine designed in 1917 confirms this. It is accepted that the Liberty engine is based on the Rolls-Royce Eagle engine, which we scrapped after the last war. We are not trying to press the claims of the Meteor engine; we should be delighted if we could be shown an engine which could replace it, and which could be produced. As no such engine exists we foresee that in 1943 large quantities of Meteor engines will be required for tanks and now is the time that this should be put on a firm basis and not treated as an odd job. Our complaint at the present time with the Ministry of Supply is that the Meteor is being given no priority. The whole of the builders of tank engines appear to have all their manufacturing facilities booked up for producing Liberties. If that is the Ministry of Supply decision we do not want to criticise their policy, but it must be accepted that there will be very few Meteor engines in 1943. . . .

It is necessary that the engine which is being developed essentially as a tank engine should be allocated a parent factory. This is not with the intention of Rolls-Royce dropping the job – we recognise that our help will be required the whole time. The reason we want a factory allocated to the Meteor is to bring home to the Ministry of Supply the fact that there is such an engine and that it does require facilities in order to produce it.

A full discussion of the position took place at the Ministry of Supply on 30 December. At this meeting Hives made it quite clear that because of the increased demands for the Merlin, due to the bomber programme and the success of the two-stage engines, there was no hope of Rolls-Royce increasing the production facilities allocated to the Meteor. It was decided, therefore, that Meadows should parent the engine but that the existing order should stand, with Rolls-Royce responsible for the delivery of the first 500 engines in 1942 and the next 500 by June 1943. Rolls-Royce was to act as technical parent and provide Meadows with Merlin parts and, where possible, assist Meadows to obtain sub-contract capacity. In particular Rolls-Royce agreed to be responsible for crankshaft supplies.

On the question of delivering 500 engines in 1942 Hives committed himself very heavily despite the experience of 1941. There was no reason to anticipate that Meadows would not be able to achieve a substantial output by the end of the year. On 1 January he informed G. C. Usher that he had no doubt about the delivery of the first five hundred engines in 1942. He was much more concerned about ensuring continuity of production. These proceedings were reported to Lord Beaverbrook, who apparently received the impression that Rolls-Royce had now accepted full responsibility for the project – quite contrary to the impression which Hives had been endeavouring to create. He cabled in a eulogistic vein from Washington expressing profound admiration of Hives' decision to assume this additional burden.

Despite these decisions, there was little improvement in the position in the early part of 1942. On 10 January H. Royce, one of the

Rolls-Royce Tank Division engineers, reported that no progress was being made at the Meadows factory. This was partly explained by lack of material but the real explanation was the lack of force and definition in the policy of the Ministry of Supply. Though a large number of tools had been delivered Meadows had not started machining any of the special pieces for the first 500 engines. A Ministry of Supply official who visited the works on 31 January was unable to clarify the situation. He 'did not know', Royce commented in his report, 'whether more than 50 engines per week were required and certainly there was no evidence that they were prepared to displace the Liberty engines.' No decision had been taken on the specification of the subsequent 1000 Mk. III engines and it did not appear that the Ministry were prepared to allot machining facilities for the Mk. II to replace the Liberty. The exact nature and extent of the responsibility was still not clear to Meadows and Royce could see no satisfactory alternative to Rolls-Royce assuming full production as well as technical responsibility. The month of February saw no improvement in the position, especially as regards the production of special pieces, and on 2 March 1942 Hives pointed out to Usher that the Meteor still appeared to have no priority whatever in the Ministry of Supply factories. It was not until 4 March 1942 that the engine was at last given A1 priority at Meadows. But even this step failed to produce any significant results. One of the principal reasons for the vacillation on the part of the Ministry of Supply at this stage was the prospect of obtaining large numbers of tank-engines from the United States, including a tank-engine produced by the Packard Company which would closely resemble if not duplicate the Meteor.

In October 1941 the Ministry of Supply instructed the British Purchasing Commission in Washington to explore the possibility of obtaining 4000 tank-engines. The first proposal was that some American manufacturer should produce the Liberty. The Packard Company was approached and they proposed to produce their early water-cooled aircraft engine, originally manufactured in 1927, as an improvement on the Liberty which they could supply without great trouble. This would obviously have been a wasteful and retrograde step and J. M. Reid, the Rolls-Royce representative at Packards, handed over the weight analysis and descriptive handbook of the Meteor to the Packard engineers. Soon afterwards Maurice Olley suggested to them that they should produce a cast-iron version of the Meteor which could be manufactured in the motor-car plant. This was done immediately and the engine was submitted to Mr Knudsen for his approval. A Lend-

Lease requisition for 5000 engines was obtained by the British Purchasing Commission but this required Knudsen's sanction before it became effective.

In January 1942 S. E. Blackstone visited Detroit and Washington to discuss the progress of this project. He found that the Packard Meteor was a considerable modification of the Rolls-Royce Meteor and embodied several features of their marine engine. Its potential power output was 900 horsepower. It was not interchangeable with the Meteor and was too different from the Packard Merlin to employ sub-standard Merlin parts in its production. The Packard Company approved of this engine and considered that it could be produced without prejudice to Packard Merlin output. They estimated that it could produce 1425 in 1942. But the management was not prepared to proceed with the engine unless it had the full backing of the U.S. army and an A1A priority. Nor would they produce any engine for which they did not have the final responsibility for design.

Neither of these conditions was fulfilled and Mr Knudsen did not favour the project. He considered that an engine of aircraft type was unsuitable for production on existing machines in a Detroit motor-car plant. The U.S. Army proposed to standardise three liquid-cooled engines for tanks – a Ford 8-cylinder, two coupled General Motors diesels and five coupled Chrysler engines – and he proposed that the Packard Company should make the Ford tank engine for the U.S. Army. There was also some opposition to the scheme from within the British Purchasing Commission on the grounds that the Packard management would not be able to handle the project without prejudice to Merlin output. It was also felt by some of the U.S. Army tank officials with whom Blackstone discussed the proposal that it was wasteful to tool up separately for the production of two engines which were so nearly alike. The basic problem in the United States was different from that in England. In England the idea was to employ as many Merlin pieces as possible in the production of the engine, whereas in America the object was to employ the productive capacity of the machinery already existing in Detroit to the best advantage. It was felt that the Packard proposal had arrived six months too late and from this point of view it was unfortunate that Packards had not been informed of the general trend of Meteor development in England. One of Blackstone's first conclusions on examining the tank situation in the United States was that insufficient information, based on battle experience in Europe and Africa, was being made available in the United States. The U.S. Army tank authorities finally agreed to support the engine if Packards would agree to its being taken over as a joint proposition by the leading car manufacturers, but when the increased Packard Merlin orders came through in June 1942 the proposal was completely abandoned.

It was known that the Ford Company had successfully developed a 600 h.p. V-8 tank engine which was a cut-down version of a 12-cylinder Ford aircraft engine based on the Merlin. This engine was considered to be much easier to produce than the Meteor. The various tank-engine missions in the United States during 1942 pressed for the use of Ford engines in British tanks but the proposal was ultimately rejected in favour of the Meteor on the grounds that the adaptation of this type of engine to British tanks was difficult and that the figure of horsepower per ton should on no account be allowed to fall. The British Purchasing Commission therefore turned its attention to the problem of supplementing British production of the Meteor by the supply of machine tools and parts (particularly crankshafts) from the United States. G. C. Usher had gone over to America to expedite these supplies and on 20 March he cabled Hives that he was arranging for firms manufacturing Liberty crankshafts to change over to Meteor crankshafts as soon as possible. He also asked to be kept informed of any other shortages.

Things appeared to be moving at last and at a Ministry of Supply meeting on 29 April the allocation of a group of factories to Meteor production was discussed. This comprised the two Vauxhall factories and the Morris and Leyland group. Rolls-Royce agreed to parent this group and to start a development factory at Burton for the cast-iron Meteor. It was decided at this meeting that there was no point in relying to any large extent on Meadows, who had still shown no enthusiasm for the work which they had been asked to do. In consequence, the Ministry decided to abandon the proposed extensions to the Meadows plant. Production was nevertheless to continue on the existing scale.

At this meeting J. D. Crozier stated that the total tank-engine requirements for 1944 were now 20,000 engines, practically all of which were Meteor. Hives still expected as late as March that 500 engines would be produced in 1942 but this new figure required an increase in production from 160 a month in December 1942 to 1600 a month in January 1944. If the rate of expansion of aero-engine production was to be any guide, this clearly demanded a clear policy and the most strenuous efforts on the part of all concerned. Surprisingly enough, this comparison never seems to have been made.

In the meantime the Tank Division at Belper had continued with its development work which had gradually been extended to the whole tank. This resulted in the 'Cromwell' tank, a design which was standardised for quantity production in 1943. The general design and development position was discussed by Robotham in a memorandum to Hives on 26 May. This pointed out that the major cause of the unreliability of existing tanks had been production 'off the drawing-board' and the lack of development facilities. 'We are gradually building up other cells throughout the country where development work is proceeding on various tank components, but supervisory talent is so scarce that we frequently find it easier to do the work ourselves than to guide, from a distance, people who are not always willing to do what we want. . . . The responsibility for the conception of better tanks for the future at present rests with Belper to quite an appreciable extent.'

13. A Cromwell tank being inspected by Winston Churchill

Robotham, who had been appointed Chief Engineer of Tank Development and was thus given official status outside Rolls-Royce, now began to apply the general principles of rationalisation which he had developed for the Rolls-Royce and Bentley cars to the design and production of tanks. His programme, which was backed by the Ministry of Supply, was to develop new tanks with varying ranges of armour and armament, all of which could be manufactured from a standard set of components. Four tanks were under development at Belper – the Mk. VIII or Cromwell III, the A.30 with a 17-pounder gun, an intermediate assault tank (a heavy Cromwell) and an assault Cromwell of 42 tons. Belper had assumed responsibility for all the components of these vehicles. At the end of July two of these tanks were demonstrated to members of the General Staff, including General Sir Alan Brooke, who expressed astonishment at the progress which had been made.

Though the first production engine was put on test at the Meadows factory on 28 March 1942, it had become increasingly obvious that no real production could be expected from this factory. Several criticisms had been set out in a Rolls-Royce memorandum to Meadows, and this had naturally caused some resentment. Very little further progress was made at this factory during the summer and autumn of 1942. The Ministry of Supply was more concerned with organising Meteor and Cromwell production on a large scale for 1943 and 1944 than in ensuring the output promised for 1942, and consequently not much notice was taken of this lamentable failure until towards the end of the year.

On 21 May the final decision to allocate the Vauxhall group to the Cromwell was taken. This necessarily involved a large-scale switch from the Liberty to the Meteor and the fact that it was decided to keep this decision secret in order to avoid a slackening of effort at firms producing the Liberty illustrates the peculiarly difficult psychological problems which are involved in the centralised administration of industrial production, even in time of war.

On 17 June the conversion of Vauxhall capacity was discussed at Luton and it was decided that a programme of 50 Meteors a week would involve a major development scheme at the Luton factory owing to the general unsuitability of the existing plant. The whole subject was fully discussed between representatives of the Ministry of Supply, Rolls-Royce and Vauxhalls at Derby on 21 June. At this meeting it was decided to produce the Meteor I (aluminium Meteor) since the Meteor X was not sufficiently developed and Vauxhalls wished to take advantage of the proved production methods in the Merlin group.[6] The possibility of introducing the Meteor X at a later date was dismissed. An output of 200 engines per week was estimated to require 375,000 sq. ft. of factory space and a further 3500 employees.

H. Royce, who had had considerable experience of the problems at Meadows, was sceptical of the Vauxhall scheme. He recommended that either Rolls-Royce or Vauxhalls should accept full responsibility for production with the other acting as sub-contractor. A further proposal was that Vauxhalls should be responsible for a limited number of items and for assembly and test, the rest being provided by Rolls-Royce and sub-contractors.

For a variety of reasons the Vauxhall scheme did not materialise and the main expansion during the summer was confined to the acquisition of sections of two factories in Nottingham by the development organisation at Belper. The success of tank production appeared to be inversely proportional to the speed of tank development. In August the position became so desperate that the Ministry of Aircraft Production was prepared to release 300 Merlin XXs for conversion to Meteors as a special concession. This offer was not accepted since the shortage was occasioned by the failure to produce the special Meteor parts. Production of these parts was just starting at the Meadows factory and at a Ministry of Supply meeting held on 8 August Hives pointed out that the Ministry would be fortunate if 200 engines, produced by what he described vividly as 'knife and fork methods', were to be made available in 1942. Machine tools were in desperately short supply and this was undoubtedly one factor holding up the Meadows expansion. There was also a severe shortage of Meteor castings owing primarily to the failure of the Ministry of Labour to provide the additional men required to increase production at the Hillington foundry.

In September 1942 a Commander A. R. Micklem became Chairman of the Tank Board and he immediately appointed a committee to investigate Meteor production. This committee consisted of S. E. Blackstone, J. C. Blair from the Directorate of Machine Tools, and C. J. Brown, the Deputy Director of Tank Supply. The committee's directive instructed them to contact the Rover, Austin, Leyland, Vauxhall, Meadows, Rolls-Royce and Nuffield companies with a view to expediting the production of the Meteor and enlarging the capacity for its production.

Before beginning their investigation the committee agreed that the essential basis of an expansion scheme, or even a major sub-contract scheme, was the acceptance of production and assembly responsibility by a major factory. To achieve the production figures contemplated for 1944 would involve a major changeover at any of these factories and since this was dependent on the supply of machine tools, which were unlikely to be made available before the last quarter of 1943, it was obvious that no large increase in production could be expected in 1943.

Rolls-Royce was clearly not prepared to accept such a liability. Nor did the committee consider that the Meadows Company would make a suitable parent. Their record in 1942 had not impressed the committee, which considered that if this company was chosen as parent it was 'imperative that they be relieved of the large and varied programme they have on their books of general combustion engine manufacture'. The key to this company's failure to produce the Meteor was to be found in their absorption in other work.

The Vauxhall proposal had been rejected by the Ministry of Supply because of the large amount of labour, machine tools and supervision required and because the company was heavily committed to the production of army transport. The company was nevertheless prepared to provide sub-contract assistance. The Engine Branch of the Morris Company were prepared to take on the Meteor on completion of their Liberty contract at the end of 1943. This company was just completing a major changeover to Liberty production with a programme of 50 engines a week. The Rover factory was not visited by the committee, but since this company was just completing its Cheetah contract the committee recommended that the possibility of employing its capacity should be considered. The Austin Company's existing commitments were too great to allow it to consider Meteor production. The managing director, Mr L. P. Lord, complained that his planning staff was 'stretched to the limit' by the constant flow of aircraft modifications and he suggested that other companies were in a far better position to undertake the work.

The main recommendation of the committee was that the Morris Company should prepare to produce the Meteor with assistance from Leylands. It was decided that all firms other than the Morris Company producing Libertys should increase output as much as possible so that the changeover would not affect supply during 1943. A cylinder-block line was to be installed in the Armstrong-Siddeley group and existing sub-contractors used as much as possible. By September 1942 there were fifty-one sub-contractors producing Meteor components. Of these fourteen were Rolls-Royce sub-contractors, five had received tools under the Meteor grant and thirty-two had received no tools whatever.

The committee pointed out that the success of the scheme depended on the release of machine tools and labour from existing sources of Liberty production. This was hardly a surprising conclusion. If the great majority of the suitable resources for tank engine production were allocated to the production of a disastrously obsolete engine it was quite obvious that the production of a newer and more powerful engine would necessitate a ruthless suspension of this engine. The structure of the British engineering industry, both in aircraft and tanks, seemed always to encourage the abandonment of the 'either-or' principle in favour of the 'some-of-both'. The central authorities, upon whom the stringent necessity for making a firm choice and insisting on its execution devolved generally preferred to postpone decisions which would have involved ordering several firms to produce a standardised product. Given the existing structure of British industry there was naturally a limit to the extent to which rationalisation could have been enforced without seriously affecting current output. In time of war no country can 'take six months off' while it reorganises its factories, but in the production of tank engines the rigidities of outlook and structure were particularly costly in terms of wasted resources and loss of life on the battlefield because of inferior equipment.[7]

The problem of rationalisation was discussed by the committee, which came to the following conclusion:

> It is considered that a useful amount of capacity in the form of personnel, factory space and plant could be released for the engine scheme if the varied manufacture of standard engines in the motorcar factories throughout the country were rationalised and confined to one or two works. In other words it is considered that too many varied and miscellaneous engines are now being made in too many different places and a rationalisation of this would throw up a considerable amount of engine capacity.[8]

This revolutionary proposal received no serious consideration. The remaining recommendations of the committee were acted upon, however, and by the end of the year it had been decided that the Meteor would continue in production at the Meadows factory and that the Morris engine factory at Coventry, and the Rover factory at Tyseley, would convert to Meteor production during the course of 1943. Fewer than 200 engines were delivered from the Meadows factory during 1942 but Hives felt that his promise had been contingent upon the supply of the necessary tools and capacity and that he could not therefore be held responsible for the failure. This was not strictly true, though the general responsibility for the low output of Meteors could not be laid at Rolls-Royce's door. The delivery of machine tools was not as rapid as had been hoped for but most of these tools were diverted into aero-engine production. The contribution of parts from both the Glasgow and Derby factories was substantially less than the output which would have been justified in terms of the machine-hours which these tools made available. Total deliveries from Derby amounted to only 13 per cent of the theoretical figure. But the failure to supply parts in the promised quantities to the Meadows factory was not responsible for the low output of this factory, and it would have been pointless to accumulate large stocks of Merlin-Meteor parts when these could not be used in the Meteor, and when the demand for the Merlin was as great as ever.

By the beginning of 1943, however, the position had become final-ised and though the 1943 output of the Meteor was still almost entirely dependent on the Rolls-Royce-Meadows group, the main responsibility for production in 1944 was to rest on the Rover and Morris factories. Thus, by the beginning of 1943 most of the main technical and production problems had been solved, not least because of the consid-erable contribution from Rolls-Royce.

During 1943 production got under way at all three factories and the only problems confronting Rolls-Royce were those of technical paren-tage. Complications developed from the fact that the parentage of the Cromwell (Meteor) and Centaur (Liberty) tanks had been entrusted to the Leyland Company in May 1943. The Leyland Company continued to press the Ministry of Supply to allow them to develop the Liberty despite all the accumulated experience of this engine's performance in 1941 and 1942. This was all the more surprising in view of the fact that the Liberty had been giving trouble and had caused considerable concern at the Ministry of Supply, and even more especially in view of the opinion of the Army authorities that the Cromwell III was the best tank that had ever been through their hands.

Hives was annoyed by this interference, which was affecting Meteor production, and complained bitterly to Commander Micklem.

We have neither the desire nor the intention, and certainly not the time, to justify the Merlin design for the Meteor engine to Leylands. I do not profess to understand the duties of parent firms on tanks, but we have a very accurate knowledge of what is required on the service of engines. . . . As you will appreciate a considerable amount of time is spent by our people in giving information to Rovers and Morris'; we have accepted this, on the understanding that they were going to be responsible for the Meteor engine. If on top of that you are going to superimpose another parent, who is in a position to dictate policy, then I'm afraid we are only left with two alternatives – (1) a sit-down strike, and (2) to decide that in spite of the Ministry of Supply or the nominated parent, we shall go flat out to make a success of the Meteor engine, and the Cromwell as far as it is possible.

Commander Micklem immediately arranged a meeting at which Hives was able to straighten the whole matter out and to convince the Ministry and Leylands that the responsibility for the engine had to be precisely located. Rolls-Royce continued to be parent until the end of 1944 and the Leyland Company was instructed not to proceed any further with Liberty and Meteor tests. Specific instructions were issued to Leylands that the Meteor and no other engine was to be installed in the Cromwell.

As early as January 1943 Hives had suggested that the Rover Company should take over the technical parentage of the Meteor in the Rover-Morris-Meadows group. This was not practicable at that time since the Rover Company had its hands full in building up production alone, but the transfer was eventually made in November 1943.

The chequered history of the Meteor engine illustrates the overriding importance of a clear and definite policy which enables responsibility to be allocated precisely between two or more organisations which are collaborating on a particular project. This is especially important if development and production responsibility are to be separated, and even more so if the production responsibility itself is to be shared. Indeed it is doubtful if responsibility for the *same* undertaking can be shared. The usual result in such a case seems to be that nothing gets done and each organisation feels quite justified in blaming the other. This seems particularly likely to happen if, for whatever reason, the responsibility is only accepted with reluctance on the one side.

The main problem in 1943 occurred towards the end of the year when an acute shortage of single-piece blocks developed, but this was satisfactorily solved by dismantling surplus Merlins of the older marks. Following the Merlin a two-piece block Meteor had been developed at Belper and in due course this engine came into production at Rovers. Technical parentage of this later model engine was retained by Rolls-

Royce until January 1944 when it too was transferred to Rovers.

The vicissitudes of programming for the Meteor output in 1943 and 1944 were not dissimilar from those which have already been discussed in connection with aero-engine programmes. Expectations were invariably optimistic and had to be revised downwards, especially in the early months of 1943. In due course, however, production gradually caught up with the programmes,[9] whose downwards revisions became less and less drastic. In the early months of 1943 the engine output, small as it was, was considerably in excess of the output of tank hulls. This corresponded with the experience of aero-engines and airframes for ultimately by the end of 1943 the position had been reversed.

Rolls-Royce may thus claim at least part of the credit for the fact that the British armoured divisions which invaded Europe in 1944 were equipped with a first-class tank worthy of the name. Had it not been for the firm's willingness to undertake the 'preliminary' responsibility in 1941 and to continue to carry the more vexatious responsibilities which had to be borne in 1942 and 1943, which could easily have been shifted on the grounds of aero-engine priority, the British Army would either have had to rely on American tanks or to use tanks engined by the Liberty, an engine whose potentialities had long been exhausted. For this work the company received no financial reward whatsoever, the entire project being financed through the Glasgow imprest account, and very little publicity. In this, as in many other fields, a private organisation showed a remarkable capacity for appreciating and serving the highest interests of the country. This capacity would seem to depend on the ideals, enterprise and ability of the men who serve an organisation rather than the formal obligations imposed on it by title deeds which decide whether it should be regarded as a 'public' or 'private' institution. Whether, of course, such men are or can be nurtured in anything except a private enterprise environment is an interesting question which will probably never be answered while the collectivist systems are able, as a whole or in part, to draw on the brash vigour and inventiveness which the free enterprise system, whatever its other faults may be, undoubtedly encourages and makes freely available through its immense technical literature.

8 The Years of Victory, 1942–1945

The victory of the Battle of Britain and the proof which the events of 1941 provided that British industrial production was capable of withstanding the gradually diminishing power of the enemy's bombing offensive brought about a realisation that the Empire would have to plan for a war of attrition. Such a war could be won only by the most effective use of the resources at its command. During 1940 the immediate demands made by the intensity of the struggle made it necessary to waste in order to win. In 1941, though the struggle was no less intense, the war did not move spasmodically in favour of either side, and the administrative machine began, necessarily, to develop and to reassert itself. Current, rather than voltage, was now required to ensure victory. The elimination of the great uncertainties which existed in 1940 and 1941 made it possible for production to be both anticipated and directed more intelligently.

Late in 1941 the Cabinet decided to enlarge the heavy bomber programme with a view to attaining a front-line strength of 4000 heavy bombers by July 1943. This figure required a production of 22,000 aircraft of which it was expected that 5500 would be supplied from the United States. Such a figure necessarily involved a substantial increase in the output of engines, and in particular of engines from the Rolls-Royce group of factories. The Lancaster had shown early promise of being the most successful heavy bomber of the war and it was intended to be engined almost entirely by the Merlin. Several other aircraft were converted to Merlins when it was shown that this improved their performance, and several new aircraft were designed around Merlin or Griffon engines. The Rolls-Royce group alone obviously could not be expected to supply all the engines which this increased airframe output required and it was decided that a 20 per cent increase in the output of the group was the maximum which could be attained even under the most favourable conditions. The Packard

116

Merlin production in the United States was beginning to build up and it was expected that 1600 of these engines would be available in 1942 and a very much greater number in 1943 and 1944. Early in 1942 a further order for 14,000 Packard Merlins was placed with the Packard Company.

Hives did not doubt that this 20 per cent increase in the output of the Rolls-Royce group could be obtained provided that the necessary tools and labour were supplied. He estimated that it would require a total of 2000 tools, spread over the Rolls-Royce factories alone (excluding Fords) and an increase of 10,000 in the labour force. He did not think that an increase in plant capacity was necessary, and in this he was strongly supported by Lord Beaverbrook, now Minister of Supply, who

14. The Avro Lancaster Bomber

thought that a great deal of engine capacity was being wasted, particularly in the production of the Sabre. These estimates were accepted, and though it was realised that the provision of 2000 machine tools for the Rolls-Royce group and a further 1100 for the Ford factory would place a very great strain on the machine tool industry, arrangements for their supply were immediately made. The tools did not come forward as rapidly as was expected, but in due course all those originally promised were supplied.

A variety of estimates, all of which emerged in the form of programmes, were made of the increase in output which it was hoped these measures would provide. In February 1942, it was expected that the output of engines from the Rolls-Royce group (excluding Fords) would be 18,320 engines in 1942 and 22,860 in 1943. On 5 March this was revised downwards to 17,055 and 20,470 as a result of a clearer appreciation of some of the factors involved, particularly the rate of supply of machine tools and labour. The planners at the M.A.P. were in the unpleasant position of having to compromise between the unrelenting demands of the Prime Minister that the bomber programme had to be met and the almost equally uncompromising realism of the engine firms, whose executives pointed out that a great deal of the increase of tool capacity was being absorbed in producing a constant output of engines whose performance and quality, and therefore mechanical complexity and cost in real terms, was steadily increasing.

The instability in the programmes, and in the output which was supposed to correspond to them, arose largely from the fact that accurate predictions could not be made of the date on which production could start and of the rate at which it would increase. Such predictions as were made were invariably optimistic by anything from six months to two years. Once a developed engine became established in production in one or more factories, the prediction of output became a relatively straightforward matter, but until this stage was reached an informed guess was the most that could be expected.

With the newer engines, however, this could not be done. The output of the newer marks of Merlin and Griffon in 1942, 1943 and 1944 was invariably below expectations and a source of disappointment to the Ministries, especially when their guesses had become invested with moral overtones. This applied particularly to the Merlin with two-stage two-speed superchargers and two-piece blocks. The first Merlin of this series, the Merlin 61, was such an outstanding success that the Air Ministry authorised an immediate production order before the type-test

15. The Rolls-Royce V-12 cylinder Griffon

had been completed. It was installed in a new mark of high-altitude Spitfire which was urgently required by Fighter Command early in 1942 to meet the challenge of the Focke-Wulf 190 fighter, a superb machine which completely outclassed the older mark of Spitfire. The development of the Merlin 60 series of engines had been given priority late in 1941 and in consequence work on the Griffon had suffered and this engine was not brought into production at Derby in any appreciable quantity until 1943. Even in this year only 396 were produced. This figure was raised to 1257 in 1944. But the new mark of Merlin had such an improved performance that the Griffon, in its early stages, had a very small margin of performance to commend it. This again justified Hives's policy that the industry should develop known rather than unknown engines. A further argument in favour of this policy was the fact that the factories were also familiar with the production problems of the known engine and it was always easier to introduce even a substantial modification such as a two-speed supercharger to an engine already in production than to introduce a completely new engine such as the Griffon or Vulture.

The output of the group in 1942 nevertheless did not fall very far below expectations in so far as the grand total of engines was concerned, although there was a constant demand for the latest types, especially from Fighter Command. The Rolls-Royce factories produced 17,400 engines and with the output of Merlin XXs from the Ford factory this provided a total of 21,300. The peak output for all four factories during 1942 was achieved in October when over 2000 engines were produced. The single-stage Merlin XX was the main engine manufactured during 1942 and Fords and Glasgow provided the majority of these. But towards the end of the year it became apparent that the output of the Rolls-Royce factories could not be expected to increase very much beyond these figures. All three Rolls-Royce factories produced just under 6000 complete engines, and though a considerable increase was expected from the Ford factory, this was to be obtained only if no change in mark was introduced.

During 1943 the production at the Rolls-Royce factories increased slightly to 18,800 while the production at Fords almost doubled, reaching a total of 6900. But this again was largely explained by the fact that whereas the Ford factory confined itself to the Merlin XX series both Derby and Crewe were faced with the problem of introducing two-stage Merlin production. The Derby factory was also producing the Griffon during 1943 and towards the end of the same year Crewe began to make preparations for its introduction. The production effort at Glasgow in 1942 and 1943 was in fact much greater than the figures for complete engines (5750 and 6576) reveal. In 1942 Rolls-Royce agreed to accept responsibility for the Packard Merlin engines which were beginning to arrive in England for installation in the Lancaster and other aircraft. The first batch of these engines, though they were excellent from all other points of view, required one important modification to the connecting rods which involved extensive dismantling and rebuilding. The engines also lacked a variety of installation fittings which through some oversight had not been ordered when the original order for the first 6000 engines was placed. This deficiency was remedied in all subsequent orders, but in 1942 and 1943 the engines could not have been installed in British aircraft had Rolls-Royce not agreed to carry out the modifications arranged for the manufacture of the supplementary items. The supplies of Packard engines in 1942 were not as great as the M.A.P. had originally expected, but in 1943 no

16. The North American P51D Mustang with Packard Merlin

less than 5261 Packard Merlins were rectified at Glasgow. The output of repaired engines at this factory was also substantial.

The maximum effort of the group was attained in 1944 when a total of 28,2000 engines was produced, including 10,100 from the Ford factory. The actual quantitative totals from the three Rolls-Royce factories were lower by a few hundred engines in 1944 than in 1943 at each factory, but the production effort was much greater since the more complicated Merlins and the Griffon required a far larger number of machining-hours in their production than the simpler marks of engine. The comparative output of Derby is all the more impressive in view of the fact that in 1943 no less than fifteen marks of Merlin, ranging from the Merlin 20 to the Merlin 73, and seven marks of Griffon were produced at the Derby factory. In 1944 this had been reduced to eight marks of Merlin, though the number of marks of Griffon remained the same. The Crewe factory was also obliged to produce a large variety of engine (fifteen marks of Merlin in 1943) and in 1944 the Griffon was introduced at this factory as well. There had been hopes of a substantial supply of the two-stage engine from the United States as soon as the Packard Company had developed its production of this engine, but Packards did not prove any more capable than the parent organisation of changing rapidly from the production of the earlier to the later types. The production of two-stage engines was therefore started at Glasgow in 1944 as an insurance.

From a production point of view the problem would have been greatly simplified if the demand for the older marks of engines had declined as that for the newer marks increased. This never happened and the considerable lag was as much an indication of the remarkable rate of Merlin development as it was an indication of the reluctance of M.A.P. officials to risk a shortage of any mark of engine. When 'maximum production' is looked upon as one of the main objectives in wartime, the mere quantitative totals appear at times to have a mesmerising effect and the intrinsic and ever-changing relationship between quantity and quality has frequently to be rediscovered. The process of rediscovery often seems to involve a considerable waste of resources. Thus towards the end of the war large surpluses of the earlier marks of Merlin began to accumulate and the apparatus of control did not prove as responsive as might have been expected by this time. There was no equivalent of the 'market' response to surplus or obsolescence. The output of two-stage engines and Griffons from Derby and Crewe would have been substantially greater in 1943 and 1944 had these factories not been obliged to carry the burden of producing simultaneously several other marks of Merlin to supplement the output of the other two factories. In many respects the very flexibility of the Derby factory in particular proved its own undoing from the quantity production point of view. This was especially the case when the R.A.F. suddenly discovered that one of its aircraft flew better with a Merlin and asked for Merlins to be installed.[1] At worst this required the production of a special engine (when the demand was for a particular type of performance), at best it required the modification of an existing mark to such an appreciable extent that the engine became virtually a new mark. The production of such an engine with its minor, but from a production point of view extremely important, peculiarities at one of the mass-production factories would have involved great dislocation of machines and methods and consequently the work had to be undertaken by the two factories where flexible techniques had been maintained. The cost of this flexibility does not always seem to have been clearly appreciated either at the M.A.P. or the Air Ministry. But when the need arose the superiority which it conferred on R.A.F. fighters was very substantial.

During 1942 and 1943 there was a much greater measure of agreement between the management and the Ministries. From time to time the M.A.P. continued to make extravagant demands in its programmes but under the influence of Sir Wilfrid Freeman, who returned to the M.A.P. as Chief Executive late in 1942, a stronger sense of the limitations of statistics and of the practical significance of the programme was induced in M.A.P. officials. On the question of engine development Hives had undoubtedly won, and proved, his point. As far as reciprocating engines were concerned the Ministries did not again lose faith in the potentialities of the Merlin. The development of this remarkable engine continued into the Merlin 100 series which employed petrol-injection instead of the old type of carburation. The more hopeful production targets were not hit, especially in the later marks of engine and at one stage in 1943 – one of the few occasions during the war on which it was necessary to do so – Spitfires were ferried with slave engines. This occurred while Hives was in America on tour of the American aircraft industry and Sir Wilfrid Freeman asked the Chairman, Lord Herbert Scott, to use his personal influence to improve two-stage Merlin production. Lord Herbert Scott referred the matter to the managing director, who ordered a full investigation. This revealed that the firm could not altogether be blamed for what had happened.

In some respects, as Sidgreaves admitted to the chairman, the firm had tied its own noose. 'I am afraid', he said, 'that our enthusiasm and zeal to introduce new types has been greater than our real ability to do so. In other words we set ourselves too difficult a target because of our enthusiasm to give the R.A.F. the very best and latest engines at the earliest possible moment.' Sidgreaves considered that the firm had been too accommodating in accepting frequent changes of type in programmes from the M.A.P. and that the Ministry had almost come to take production miracles for granted. He would not accept the charge of a general shortage since production in August had exceeded absorption by 600 engines and he considered that Sir Wilfrid Freeman was exaggerating when he stated that the deficiencies were having an adverse effect upon the whole aircraft programme. 'We know the position pretty well', he remarked, 'and can say that so far we have

17. The de Havilland Mosquito BIV

managed to keep the aircraft constructors all going fully with engines, with the possible exception of a small shortage of the particular type of two-stage variety used in the latest Mosquito.' In a memorandum on the subject Mr Swift pointed out that the supply of tools, labour and materials had not been as great as was promised and he also considered that a contributory cause was the waste of materials and labour in the production of the older marks of engine for which the demand from the aircraft constructors was steadily diminishing. The number of marks in production had increased steadily and a great effort had been put into the production of special engines which had been ordered in small quantities and which in one case were not even used. In October 1942

Hives had told the board that the M.A.P. were unwise to expect a production of 22,500 engines in 1943, partly on account of the shortage of tools and labour but even more so because of the multiplicity of types. 'The time has arrived', he continued, 'when the M.A.P. have got to cut down the luxury articles in their programme. We know how much effort and capacity is tied up on projects which have a very doubtful value.' This warning was not heeded and the retarded evolution of the two-stage Merlin and Griffon engines was one of the principal consequences.

By the end of 1943 the liaison between the firm and the Ministries had become very close and the apparatus for dealing with production difficulties had been greatly improved. Regular meetings of technical and production committees took place and the information at their disposal was greatly improved in quality and quantity. Paradoxically enough, by the time this apparatus of co-ordination really began to work smoothly most of the main problems had been solved. Victory was now a matter of time and keeping the production machine well oiled.

9 Co-operation with Whittle

The company made one other major contribution to aircraft technology, if not to the winning of the war, during this period. This was in the sphere of jet propulsion. Jet aircraft became operational in Germany in late 1944 and even earlier than this the impact of the flying bomb had confirmed the suspicion of a rather startled public that the threat of secret weapons had to be taken seriously. In the event British jet aircraft did not become operational in any considerable numbers before the end of the European war but the fact that they did so at all was due as much to the drive which Rolls-Royce put into the development and production of the jet engine when asked by the M.A.P. to do so as it was to the brilliant pioneer work carried out by Air Commodore Whittle and the unusual and enterprising organisation which he established to carry out this scheme.

The Rolls-Royce design staff were by no means unaware of the significance and potentiality of the internal combustion turbine which forms the basis of the jet engine, and in 1939 the firm had persuaded Dr A. A. Griffith, an expert on this type of engine, to direct research at Derby in this field. Dr Griffith had been working on gas turbines at the Royal Aeronautical Establishment independently of Air Commodore Whittle for many years and as early as 1929 he had submitted a report in which he stated that the turbine was 'superior to existing service engines and to projected compression-ignition engines in every respect examined'. Unfortunately this view was not officially accepted and Dr Griffith had no opportunity of continuing to develop his ideas until 1937. Between 1930 and 1937 all the effective work on the jet engine in Britain was carried out by Air Commodore Whittle under the most adverse conditions. Work was resumed at the R.A.E. under the direction of Mr Hayne Constant and Dr Griffith in 1937 very largely because of the success of Whittle's engine. Dr Griffith favoured a jet engine with a contra-flow compressor whereas Whittle's engine employed a centrifugal compressor which in its early stages gave a great deal of trouble. The R.A.E. engineers did not have much confidence in the Whittle compressor and at one stage they recommended that official support should be withdrawn. Dr Griffith had always considered that the ultimate potentialities of the contra-flow type of compressor were far greater than those of the centrifugal compressor, and when he joined Rolls-Royce it was agreed that he should continue his work along these lines.

In the meantime Whittle had succeeded in impressing the Air Ministry sufficiently to gain financial backing for the development work which the company he had formed specially for the purpose, Power Jets Limited, wished to carry out. After the outbreak of war the gas-turbine received influential support and in due course the Air Ministry encouraged several major firms in the industry apart from Rolls-Royce – De Havilland, Armstrong-Siddeley, Vickers and Bristols – to develop engines designed basically on the Whittle principle. Rolls-Royce was thus the only firm in the aircraft industry to undertake the development of the gas turbine on its own initiative.

In backing Dr Griffith's ideas the management realised that they were backing the more difficult type of engine and in a report on the project written in June 1939 it was pointed out that Dr Griffith was of the opinion 'that the orthodox scheme of Internal Combustion Turbine is not a sufficiently promising avenue of research and that it would be wise for us to leave Metro-Vickers to show what can be done with it.' There was no doubt whatever in 1939 of the fundamental soundness of the proposal and it was considered that if the detailed mechanical problems involved in the development of a complete unit could be satisfactorily solved it would be possible to develop a turbine which would 'at least equal the petrol engine in regard to fuel consumption and which might be superior in other respects, particularly installed weight.' The magnitude of the problem was thus clearly appreciated and the failure of the Griffith type of engine to develop rapidly came as no surprise. The whole concept of one gas turbine was considered to be a long-term project from the very beginning and even in February 1942 Hives warned the board that results could not be expected for several years.

Quite apart from the eventual success of Dr Griffith's own ideas, the initiation of this work at Rolls-Royce was to prove of great importance. A great deal of experience was acquired on the peculiarities of certain features common to all types of jet engine and when an intensive drive to develop the Whittle type of turbine into an engine suitable for production was called for in 1942 and 1943 Rolls-Royce was in a good position to underwrite the responsibility for doing so.

The firm of Power Jets had neither the resources nor the experience to undertake the production of the engine which Whittle had developed and when this received the full support of the Air Ministry late in 1939 – after the successful run of the prototype had demolished the last refuge of sceptical minds – Whittle himself suggested that the Rover Company should be brought in on the production side. With the approval and backing of the Air Ministry an arrangement was made whereby Power Jets was to have full responsibility for thermo-dynamic design and development while Rovers covered the problems of mechanical and structural design for production. Because of various restrictions which had been placed upon Whittle's work the commercial position of Power Jets had been very uncertain from the start. The main assets of the Company were the designs of the Whittle engines and the technical knowledge which its engineers had developed. Power Jets were naturally not prepared to surrender these without some acceptable form of commercial agreement and the possibility of obtaining this was made even more difficult by the legal claims which the Air Ministry, by virtue of Whittle's status as a serving R.A.F. officer, felt obliged to exercise. In consequence the relationship between the two firms was made difficult from the start, and, despite many ingenious solutions which were suggested as a cure for this situation, the progress of the work inevitably suffered. Terms of collaboration were not finally settled until 1941 and it was only then that the Air Ministry was prepared to predict that the first production aircraft might be ready early in 1942. The intention was that Rovers should plan a factory on a shadow basis, and for this purpose a large woollen mill at Barnoldswick was acquired, converted and extensively equipped with machine tools at a cost of over a million pounds. In addition a completely new development section was established at Clitheroe. At an early stage the Lucas Company was brought in as a sub-contractor. The production of the aircraft for these engines was entrusted to the Gloster Company.

The Rover Company, which had little experience of the problems of aero-engine development, soon discovered that the technical production difficulties were very considerable. Practically all the problems encountered were completely novel both from the design and production point of view. Special materials had to withstand unusually high temperatures and stresses and these could not be worked by ordinary methods. In consequence special tools had to be designed and constructed and it soon became obvious that the production of the engine in any quantity was not likely to be achieved in 1941 or the early part of 1942. An already difficult problem was further complicated by the failure of the two firms to achieve the degree of co-operation which was vital to the success of an undertaking of this nature and when, as was intended by the M.A.P., the Rover Company began to carry out independent design and development work without informing Power Jets, collaboration between the two concerns ceased to be effective.

The mistake made in this arrangement was in conceiving the problem in terms of a theoretical separation between development and production at a stage when development was so continuous that the production of anything more than a small batch of prototype engines would have been a sheer waste of resources. It was inevitable that any firm 'producing' an engine of this exceedingly novel and complex character should have had to carry out as much development work as the organisation theoretically responsible for development only. The Air Ministry and M.A.P. had in effect attempted to superimpose on the development of the engine an administrative and legal division of responsibility and function which may have been excused by the desire of each organisation to preserve its independence but was certainly not justified by the nature of the work to be carried out. This was appreciated in due course but by this time the personal relationships between the two organisations had deteriorated to such an extent that the obvious solution – an amalgamation of the two firms – was out of the question.

Rolls-Royce first entered the general picture in May 1941 when Sir Henry Tizard approached Hives with a suggestion that Derby should give some assistance to Power Jets by manufacturing certain difficult parts for the Whittle engine. Hives agreed to do so but he pointed out that Rolls-Royce would not be satisfied 'just to become a maker of bits'. From this small beginning a fairly extensive degree of technical collaboration developed between Rolls-Royce and Power Jets. In August 1941 Hives suggested to Dr Roxbee Cox, Deputy Director of Scientific Research at the M.A.P., who was visiting Derby, that the development of the jet engine should be regarded as a national effort and that a committee should be formed on which all the firms and organisations engaged on the work were represented. He thought it only reasonable that if all this valuable technical knowledge was to be made available to the whole of the American aircraft industry in the interests of the allied war effort there should be as few barriers as possible to an effective interchange of information within the British aero-engine industry. This committee, which became known as the Gas Turbine Collaboration Committee, was strongly supported by Air Marshal Linnel and was duly formed under the chairmanship of Dr Roxbee Cox. The work which the Committee carried out in subsequent years was most valuable, its principal function being to serve as a clearing-house for information. Its members were unable to reach agreement on the question of patents but this problem was wisely shelved and a free and full discussion of technical problems at meetings was in no way prejudiced.

Towards the latter part of 1941 the Rolls-Royce gas turbine staff had begun to study the problem of the Whittle engines very closely and in 1942 it was agreed that Rolls-Royce and Power Jets would collaborate to produce an improved type of Whittle engine in an effort to develop an engine which was reliable and suitable for production. On 6 January 1942 R. W. Corbitt, a member of the turbine division, summarised the position in a memorandum in which he analysed the faults of the Whittle engine and suggested that Rolls-Royce should improve this engine 'as part of a national effort to get the Whittle into service'. Several basic modifications of the Whittle design were proposed as a solution to various problems which Whittle himself had not been able to solve.

On 12 January Hives wrote to Air Commodore Whittle elaborating these proposals. 'I want to impress upon you', he said, 'that this is not put forward with the intention of competing with the Whittle; it is with the sole desire of helping the national effort. We want to look upon our contribution as an extension of your existing facilities for development, both as regards technical assistance and facilities for producing pieces.' Whittle was enthusiastic about this arrangement and he replied that he was particularly pleased that Rolls-Royce had decided to make a substantial effort of this nature. He promised full collaboration from the staff of Power Jets and emphasised that he was not particularly concerned with the competitive aspects. 'You need have no fear', he wrote, 'that we shall regard it as a competitive effort – on the contrary, we have frequently advocated to the Ministry that if any other firm were to be asked to do such a thing it should be Rolls-Royce . . . the only people who had a technical staff sufficiently competent for the purpose. Hitherto other firms have been requested or allowed to undertake work on this development much beyond their capabilities (in our opinion) instead of being confined to functions for which they were fitted. This has placed a heavy load on us and created an atmosphere which in some quarters may have been interpreted as resentment of competition on our part, whereas in fact our objection has been to the uneconomical expenditure of effort, waste of time and the risks of failure and mistakes of a kind likely to bring unmerited discredit on the whole development and to cause unjustified pessimism in high quarters. We have no such misgivings in respect of any contribution you may wish to make to the project.'

This was an auspicious start and in this co-operative atmosphere substantial and unhampered progress was made with the redesign of Whittle's engine in the early months of 1942. This particular engine, the WRI, though not a great success in itself, provided a great deal of information which would not otherwise have been obtained and which enabled a solution to be found to most of the main problems on the W2/500 which was the main type of Whittle engine scheduled to be produced for the Gloster fighter in 1943.

But though Rolls-Royce managed to maintain excellent relationships with the management of both Power Jets and Rovers, this did not seem to improve the relationship between these two companies and for various reasons which are not relevant to this narrative production showed little signs of starting at the Barnoldswick factory. By the end of 1942 the position was becoming serious and the M.A.P. decided that the most suitable arrangement would be for Rovers to hand over its jet engine development and factories to Rolls-Royce and to undertake the production of the Meteor tank engine in its main factory. The M.A.P. also proposed that Rolls-Royce should take over Power Jets, and this was agreed to by the new Minister of Aircraft Production, Sir Stafford Cripps, but Power Jets had no particular wish to lose their independence as a company and in any case Rolls-Royce considered that they set too high a valuation on their assets. The Rover transfer was nevertheless completed satisfactorily and from most points of view the arrangement was a wise one for all concerned. Power Jets were strongly in favour of Rolls-Royce manufacturing the engine, as J. C. B. Tinling, one of the firm's directors, pointed out in a letter to Hives on 11 November. He declared that Rolls-Royce was the best firm in the industry to produce the engine and that it was 'among the few with whom we would feel entirely happy to collaborate'.

In view of the intransigent technical problems encountered in the development of the Griffith contra-flow engine the management was anxious to press ahead in whatever direction seemed to be opening up. The firm's designers were convinced that the gas turbine was the engine of the future and that it would be wise to establish a clear lead in this field. In November 1942 Hives confessed that he had at first regarded the engine with considerable scepticism. He did not consider that it would materialise in time to be of much use in the Second World War and that valuable technical resources would be wasted in its development. This prediction proved substantially correct but it was nevertheless extraordinarily fortunate that Rolls-Royce decided to add the Whittle engine to the many heavy responsibilities which the firm was already carrying in 1942 and 1943. Within three years the work which was done at Derby established Rolls-Royce as the leading firm in the world on gas-turbine technology. This achievement was largely the result of the application to the Whittle engine of the well-tried policy of development which had yielded, and was still yielding, such magnificent results on the Merlin. In his November 1942 memorandum Hives summarised the Company's intentions.

> Our approach to the Whittle turbine was that we set out to design a turbine with a modest output, but one which would run and continue to run. Our turbine will be the heaviest and biggest and give relatively less thrust than any of the others, but we shall be disappointed if it does not run reliably and for sufficiently long periods for us to learn something about it. We can then proceed to open up the throttle: in short to follow the usual Rolls-Royce practice on development.

Hives had the greatest admiration for the work which Whittle had done and was convinced that the friendly collaboration between the two organisations would continue. He was equally convinced that the jet engine would not be properly developed until some well-established firm which had the resources and the experience undertook the responsibility. But this required time and Hives was well aware that the M.A.P. would probably expect miracles from the Barnoldswick factory as soon as Rolls-Royce had taken over. On 28 December 1942 he warned the M.A.P. that they should not expect this. The mere fact of changing the management, he alleged, would not produce results. He had no intention of changing the staff at either Barnoldswick or Clitheroe and pointed out to the Ministry that Rolls-Royce did not blame Rovers for their lack of success on the turbine project. The management was only too familiar with the magnitude of the problem which had confronted Rovers and it was hoped to achieve success primarily by changing the character of the Barnoldswick factory from a production to what Hives described, in a letter to Sir Wilfrid Freeman, as a 'development and prototype production' unit.

In April Rolls-Royce was able to report to the M.A.P. that satisfactory progress was being made at Barnoldswick. But the position of the special aircraft for these engines was not so satisfactory. It was well known to the Air Ministry and those connected with gas turbine work in the industry that the enemy had made substantial progress and that his aircraft would soon be flying in considerable numbers. In a letter to Sir Wilfrid Freeman on 19 July Hives criticised the way in which the F9/40 project had been handled by the M.A.P., which had allowed Glosters to sub-contract the machine to Standards, and Standards to sub-contract it to the S.S. Jaguar Company. 'I can quite imagine', he continued, 'the legions of officials and committees of enquiry that would be instituted if the enemy gets these machines on operations.' Hives considered that American gas-turbine development was also catching up rapidly and he did not see how Britain could maintain her lead without putting more effort into the development and production of the engine. Sir Wilfrid Freeman was not favourably impressed by this proposal to increase the resources allocated to the jet aircraft programme as a whole and deprecated what he considered to be a sacrifice of the certainty of the two-stage Merlin, which was in very short supply at this time, for the uncertainty of the jet engine. He agreed however to take steps to expedite the production of the Gloster Meteor and to do what he could to improve the skilled labour position at Barnoldswick. Hives had argued that if significant production of the jet engine was expected resources additional to Barnoldswick would have to be provided. Sir Wilfrid Freeman considered that the best solution to this was to increase the Merlin output of Glasgow so that Derby could undertake more jet engine production.

Despite these difficulties production in reasonable quantities began at Barnoldswick in the middle of 1943 and though the output of the factory was never substantial compared with that of the Merlin factories it was sufficient to engine the Meteor airframes whose production did not reach appreciable proportions until early in 1944. Production of engines and airframes increased steadily during 1944 as a result of the Air Staff decision to employ jet fighters in the war against Japan and intensive development work on both the Whittle type of engine and Rolls-Royce contra-flow engine continued at Derby and Barnoldswick. In due course the contra-flow engine was successfully developed but the subsequent history of these engines does not fall within the scope of this book.[1]

10 Preparing for Peace

Rolls-Royce's contribution to the development of the jet engine was the final phase, chronologically, of the company's war effort. By the spring of 1944 the maximum effort had been made and though all four of the main engine factories continued in full production until December the problems which now became the concern of the policy-makers were those of peace rather than war. The vast expansion in output, in the scope of the company's activity and in the physical resources at its disposal were somewhat surprising even to the management. Quite early on in the war the board had begun to discuss the difficulties of reconversion and the nature and extent of the markets which Rolls-Royce might expect to supply in the post-war period. There was no doubt whatever of the company's status in the eyes of the State. With a record that was unsurpassed Rolls-Royce emerged from the Second World War, as it had from the First, well ahead of every aero-engine firm both in Great Britain and the United States in the fields which it had chosen and made its own. Sir Wilfrid Freeman made a serious point when he suggested in June 1945 that a baronetcy should be conferred on the firm for its services in the cause of freedom. 'No firm', he said, 'or people, have done more in this country to achieve air superiority than have Rolls-Royce and its staff.' Its commercial integrity was as unquestioned as its technical authority and independence were widely respected.[1]

The board thus had no reason to question the fact that the R.A.F. would continue to rely on Rolls-Royce. The big question which had to be decided was whether or not Rolls-Royce intended to rely completely on the R.A.F. This depended on the answer to several questions. Would there be a civil market for the type of aero-engine which the company produced, would this market be substantial, would there be a civil market for the jet engine, would there be any market at all for the product on which the firm had originally made its name and with which it was still very largely associated in the eyes of the general public? The board had no wish to become completely dependent on the State since this would undoubtedly in due course involve the loss of that independence of judgement which had stood the country in such good stead during the war years – years when it might easily have been lost had Rolls-Royce not been led by men who were prepared to back their private judgement of the public interest against the judgement of those who often acted as though the quality of their decisions was enhanced if not sanctified by the fact that they occupied some official position in the hierarchies of the State.

Hives had fairly clear ideas on these subjects as early as 1940. He pointed out that the company had made a big mistake after the First World War in allowing aero-engine development to be seriously cut down. This policy had given other firms in the industry a chance to catch up, with consequences which might easily have become serious. There was no need to repeat this mistake. Whatever else may have been in doubt there was now no question whatever that the aero-engine was the major product of the company from every point of view. In a letter to Lord Herbert Scott, Hives stressed the fact that the management's principal task after the war was to maintain the supremacy of the firm in the aero-engine field. On no account should the motor-car business be allowed to jeopardise this. Four years later this had become not so much a question of the relative importance of motor-car and aero-engine manufacture as a question of how this enormously increased cost of aero-engine development work was to be financed. There was obviously a minimum below which indirect costs could not be reduced if the firm was to remain in a position to carry out effective development work. It was equally obvious that the production of cars could not be expected, as it had been in the twenties, to carry part of this burden since the two technologies had become almost completely differentiated. The only allocation which could now be made was that between military and civil customers.

The management had no particular wish to rush back into the production of cars but there was never any doubt that one more attempt would be made, provided the market still existed, to apply the lessons which had been learnt in the thirties. Hives considered that the Crewe factory should in due course become the car factory and that the production of motor cars should be established under a completely independent management unhampered by Derby traditions or control. At one time the formation of a separate company was considered to emphasise the complete independence of the two divisions but this proposal was not implemented for financial reasons.[2]

The management was confident that the company could profit from the lessons which had been learnt in the thirties and from the work which the design staff had carried out on rationalisation. It also believed that the company as a whole had learnt a great deal about mass-production methods which could now be put to very good use at Crewe in the production of cars. But the successful employment of these methods demanded a significant change of attitude. 'I have every confidence', said Hives, 'that we can build up an extremely profitable motorcar business. We have a complete measure of the ability and talent possessed by Morris, Fords, Standards, Leylands, Rovers and Austins. Rolls-Royce possess more talent in all departments than those firms have but we can never hope to build up a profitable motorcar business until we dismiss from our minds entirely what I call the Phantom III outlook.' The task of eliminating this outlook was entrusted to a committee of the firm's younger executives who had distinguished themselves in various ways before and during the war.[3] Both Sidgreaves and Hives felt that it would be unwise for the senior executives to carry any responsibility for the details of this work but the latter was convinced that Rolls-Royce should not make any attempt to produce an expensive chassis comparable to the pre-war Rolls-Royce or Bentley. In June 1943 he summarised his views in a detailed report to the board.

> We are faced with the fact that we are in possession of a tremendous asset in Rolls-Royce motorcars, which, if neglected will dwindle away to nothing. . . . None of the directors would desire to see the motorcar business in a similar position to what it was previous to this war. In spite of any orders that might be offered to us after that the expensive car which we produced before the war can never be a profitable undertaking.

Sidgreaves was rather more sceptical on the subject of car manufacture after the war as he believed that the market for even medium-priced cars would be precarious. Nor was he optimistic about the prospects of Crewe being able to achieve a sufficient reduction in cost to bring the rationalised Rolls-Royce and Bentley into the medium-price range. In this anticipation he proved to be right. No one, however, anticipated the imposition of a purchase tax on domestic sales in the U.K. which almost equalled the cost of production.

Robotham, whose staff were working on light carriers for the army at the end of the war, had frequently proposed that one of the most effective methods of reducing the burden of overheads on car production was for Rolls-Royce to continue as a supplier of tank engines and other engines of various kinds for the Army. The basis of the idea was that these should also be rationalised engines, modified where necessary for any special purpose. Early in 1945 Sidgreaves proposed to Sir Andrew Duncan, then President of the Board of Trade, that in view of the complete separation of the two divisions which Rolls-Royce contemplated after the war the firm had a right to be treated in the same way as other firms, such as Vickers and English Electric, which worked for all three services. 'Clearly', he pointed out, 'with the advent of the internal combustion turbine the similarity between power plants for land, sea and air propulsion largely ceases to exist so that our chassis division plant will become progressively less suitable for M.A.P. work. . . . After the war we definitely plan to work for the Army, Navy and Air Force if our products meet their requirements. We cannot see how any future considerations of national defence can do otherwise than benefit from such an arrangement.' In view of the desperate tank situation in which the country had found itself in 1941, it was expected that this would have a strong appeal. Sidgreaves also considered that if the Government wished Rolls-Royce to operate part or whole of the Glasgow factory it would be unreasonable to expect the firm to confine its activities to supplying the needs of only one government department. A similar letter was sent to Sir Stafford Cripps in which Sidgreaves mentioned that Sir Wilfrid Freeman had agreed that there was no reason why Rolls-Royce should not work for several departments. Sidgreaves later discussed the matter personally with both Duncan and Cripps and succeeded in obtaining the Minister's agreement.

On 27 February the Minister wrote to Sidgreaves confirming this offer and elaborating the terms on which it was made. The firm was required to set up three completely separate divisions each of which would concern itself solely with the needs of either the Air Ministry, the Admiralty or the Ministry of Supply. In the event of a future emergency the capacity devoted to each supply ministry was to be 'frozen' in order to avoid 'the expansion of work by any supply ministry at the cost of any other supply ministry'. Cripps believed that such a system would 'avoid all discussions and disputes in the future' and would enable the best use to be made of Rolls-Royce resources in the national interest.

This somewhat rigid classification was not adopted since it was precisely by maintaining, sometimes against considerable opposition, the right to allocate resources in as flexible a manner as possible between all the factories under direct or indirect Rolls-Royce control that the company had been able to serve the national interest so effectively. Sir Stafford Cripps's proposals involved a sacrifice of productive flexibility to administrative and financial convenience but although the management had no intention of implementing them it did not abandon hope that the Ministry of Supply in particular would not neglect the remarkable record of the company in the development and production of tank-engines.

The aero-engine market was expected to be somewhat uncertain in character mainly because of the appearance of an entirely new form of propulsion, the gas-turbine. Though its evolution had been beset by technical problems this engine appeared to be both simpler and cheaper to produce (especially in terms of man-hours) than the reciprocating engine. In June 1945 Hives warned the board that if this were so stiff competition could be expected from the other aero-engine firms, several of which had produced successful prototype engines by the end of the war. 'The very fact', he said, 'that we have been able to design an entirely new jet engine, put it on the test bed for the first time and complete a 100 hours test without looking inside it indicates that as regards jet engines they are relatively simple to design and produce, and as soon as things become simple then one must expect keen competition. Generally we rely on making difficult products where it does not pay people to compete. Fortunately the tendency on jet engines will be for them to become more complicated and therefore more difficult, which is more in our line of business.' This forecast certainly proved to be correct.

There was no doubt that the jet engine would not be used in any significant numbers for civil aircraft for some time and consequently the civil market would have to depend on the existing type of engines during this interim period. The firm had never catered extensively for this market in the past, mainly because of the fact that in the inter-war period the civil aircraft market in Europe was small compared with that in the United States. The American radial engine had predominated both in Europe and the United States since it was considered more reliable and more suitable in every way than the liquid-cooled in-line engine of the Kestrel-Merlin type. The war completely demolished the belief that the in-line engine was either unreliable or uneconomical compared with the radial, and although bigger and better radials had been developed both in Britain and the United States, Rolls-Royce saw no reason why the Merlin should not be advocated for civil aircraft. Merlins had been successfully installed in the Avro York and in 1944 an important order to install Merlins in DC-4 transport aircraft was received from the Canadian airline Canadair. There was thus no doubt that its development should continue as an engine for civil aircraft. The main problem which now faced the management was whether or not the development of other reciprocating engines should be continued. A 24-cylinder X engine (the Eagle) and a twelve-cylinder two-stroke engine (the Crecy) had been under development for some time, quite apart from the Griffon. Hives recommended that the two-stroke should be dropped as he believed M.A.P. orders for the Eagle were too small to enable the firm to gain the experience on this engine which was necessary if it was ultimately to be recommended for civil use. It was agreed therefore that the engine should be abandoned as soon as the military requirements had been completed. In view of the large number of jet engines under development and the fact that the technical staff were convinced that the jet engine would eventually displace the reciprocating engine in all major forms of air transport it was inevitable that the firm would have to limit development work on the older types of engine. In due course all Merlin production, development and repair work was transferred to the section of the Glasgow factory which the company decided to rent from the Government. It was originally intended that all other aero work, including jet engine production, should return to Derby; but after careful consideration had been given to the volume of military and civil orders the Barnoldswick factory was retained for jet engine production. It very soon became evident that most potential customers were more interested in jet engines than any other variety and within a few months of the end of the war several firms began to negotiate for a licence to manufacture the engines then in production at Derby and Barnoldswick.

Negotiations with the various interested departments of State on the problem of transferring factories or portions of factories which had been entirely financed by state capital began during 1944 when the first major reductions in output were ordered. Numerous suggestions and counter suggestions were made aimed at securing a settlement which was equitable and realistic. The full details of these negotiations and the settlements which were finally made belong rather to the history of the post-war era, but the solution achieved seemed on the whole to have been satisfactory to the company. Its financial resources had been husbanded as carefully as wartime conditions permitted in order to finance the retooling of the Crewe factory for car production, but the management was by no means certain that car production would prove a profitable venture and the risks involved in equipping and converting a large factory to produce what was virtually a new type of car were not inconsiderable. A major part of the Crewe factory was retained for this purpose and a large number of machine tools and other fittings were purchased from the Government. As far as the Glasgow factory was concerned, it was obvious from the outset that the company would not have a turnover which would enable it to employ this plant on anything like the wartime scale. The management had no intention of transferring work from either Derby or Crewe to Glasgow for the sole purpose of keeping a section of this factory employed but it was eventually decided that a section should be taken over as the parent factory for Merlin production and repairs and that this could be done without prejudicing the economic strength of the firm. The disposal of the foundry, one of the largest and most efficient of its kind in Britain, was another problem but this was solved by forming a completely new company, Renfrew Foundries, in which Rolls-Royce and Almin Ltd each invested £300,000. The foundry itself was bought outright from the Government by the new company. The agreement between the two companies gave Rolls-Royce first call on the foundry's output but it was realised that this would have to be much greater than that which Rolls-Royce's peacetime requirements alone would have justified if the plant was to achieve economical operation.

The war accentuated the division which was already taking place between the two spheres of chassis and aero production and intro-duced a third division between the reciprocating engine and the jet engine which will probably be temporary in character if, as is expected, the reciprocating engine is in due course completely superseded. The acquisition of a substantial interest in a light alloy foundry marked the legal and economic recognition of a vertical extension of production which had been brought about by the war. This was to some extent balanced by the fact that the controlling interest in Phillips & Powis had been disposed of during the war when a suitable opportunity arose. This was done primarily because the facilities at Hucknall proved more than adequate for the purposes for which Phillips & Powis was originally acquired and it was felt that the control of this company might prove more of a liability than an asset in time of peace. This judgement proved to be sound.

In both the physical and economic sense the firm's growth had been

18. The Battle of Britain memorial window

THIS WINDOW COMMEMORATES THE PILOTS OF THE ROYAL AIR FORCE
WHO, IN THE BATTLE OF BRITAIN, TURNED THE WORK OF OUR HANDS
INTO THE SALVATION OF OUR COUNTRY.

phenomenal. The post-war contraction left Rolls-Royce with four major factories to control whereas before the major expansion began in 1938, apart from sub-contracting, Derby alone had been the principal responsibility of the management. At Derby itself there had been a substantial increase in physical plant and especially in the experimental and development facilities, an expansion which reflected the greatly increased importance and scope of the aircraft engineering industry, not only had it responded to the insatiable needs of war; the growing importance and volume of civil aviation now presented a market opportunity quite different in scale from anything which had existed outside the United States in 1939.

The history of Rolls-Royce since 1945 remains to be written. The company described in this book in fact ceased to exist in 1971, but the organisation, its assets, its workforce and its great traditions were absorbed into a new nationalised organisation, Rolls-Royce (1971) Limited, as a result of the unique financial effects of a unique contract to develop yet another aero-engine, the RB211, for the Lockheed Aircraft Company in the U.S.A. This could be said to have been a final, disastrous, error of judgement by the private enterprise firm of Rolls-Royce, an error which neither Royce, Johnson, Sidgreaves nor Hives would ever have made. But who can say? These matters will be intensively studied and many different judgements will be made, about the facts, the issues and the personalities involved. This final paragraph, a mere postscript to the original study which is now being published, suggests that future historians of Rolls-Royce will find this a rich field of enquiry.

11 Reflections on the Rolls-Royce Experience

This chapter[1] will discuss the general character of economic thought and analysis employed in studying the industrial environment, the nature of this environment as revealed by this study of a large industrial concern, and the evolution in analytical technique which appears to be necessary if a wider and more thorough understanding of human behaviour in the industrial and commercial environment is ever to be obtained.

Most economists generally concern themselves with what they have defined as the economic aspects of human behaviour, and because it is obvious that those aspects of human behaviour which do not find some economic context seem to be so few, fall readily into the habit either of disregarding non-economic motives entirely, or of establishing a convenient rate of exchange between the economic and the non-economic motive. In so doing they underrate the power of those motivations of human behaviour which operate in the economic sphere but which cannot, by the wildest stretch of the axes of their charts, be regarded as the result of a rational assessment of economic advantage by the individual, whether his actions concern only himself or some organisation on whose behalf he is acting.

Two broad fields of economic thought can be distinguished. The first, and most important, concerns itself with the behaviour of the individual economic unit, and attempts to construct a complete and consistent explanation of behaviour in the economic context. The second is concerned with the broad aggregates of human behaviour — the statistically measurable economic environment which is the compound results of the behaviour of individuals and organisations. The scientific analysis of these patterns of behaviour is almost completely dependent on measurement, and from such measurement alone can useful conclusions be drawn about trends and tendencies. These conclusions provide an adequate foundation for the construction of a useful theoretical apparatus provided that the various statistical

143

criteria of accuracy, completeness, frequency of measurement, etc., are satisfied. It is an example of what Sir Robert Watson-Watt summarised so neatly as 'the goodness of measured fact'. Aggregates and rates of change of physical factors which may have considerable economic significance – population, the capacity and movements of freight cars and cargo ships, the numbers of given types of machine tools employed in a factory or a country – these can be and are measured. It is also possible to measure aggregates and rates of change of purely economic phenomena which may or may not be directly related to physical factors. Such measurements may be primary or secondary. A primary measurement, for example, may be defined as the volume of bank deposits, the revenue and expenditure figures of trading enterprises or a State department. A secondary measurement would include such things as the income of a trading enterprise or community, the cost of production of an article, the capital invested in an enterprise or industry. Such measurements are defined here as secondary because the monetary figures on which they are based depend without exception on some value judgement by the accountant or cost accountant which may be quite arbitrary within wide limits.

Value judgements may enter into primary measurements to some extent when there is some uncertainty as to whether or not to include a particular item, but such uncertainty can usually be eliminated statistically with considerable accuracy and the order of magnitude of error is comparatively small.

There is also a third type of measurement, with which the economist has only recently become familiar. These are the primarily physical indices of production volume and efficiency – man-hours, machine-tool hours, records of stock – which have been developed as instruments of control. Without these the more complex types of industrial enterprise find their purely economic or financial measurements inadequate as instruments of executive control because of the delay which occurs between the operations concerned and the appearance of the cost and financial figures which refer to them.

Both primary and secondary economic measurements are dependent upon the existence of money or money-values which relate to some process of exchange or production to which there has been an addition or subtraction of value. The economic quantities entering the process are absolute and accurately measurable. Those issuing forth from the other side are accurately measurable, but not absolute until they are so regarded for a succeeding process of production or consumption. The extent of this addition or subtraction, within limits which may be wide or narrow, depending on the nature of the process, is a matter of individual judgement. There can be no dispute about expenditure and revenue. There may be, and there very often is, considerable dispute within a productive unit about the allocation of values employed in production.

If the economist concerns himself entirely with the measurement of primary economic phenomena then he is very largely justified in disregarding the motivations of behaviour which give rise to these strictly definable physical movements of physical commodities or services and the money or money-values which represent them and facilitate their transfer. He is entitled to draw the most abstruse conclusions from the fact that the volume of money in circulation and the output of coal both increase at Christmas time. He may go further and investigate the rate at which they increase and decrease, and he may, if he wishes, connect the two series with the physical imports of crackers and dynamite, which he is justified in valuing at current prices.

But in themselves these measurements are of very little use or significance. The measurements which interest us are the secondary measurements, which however imperfect or arbitrary, give us some indication of what is happening in the economic system. It is the function of the economist not only to tell society that it is pouring money down the drain, but which drain and why. Society is interested in finding out what it is getting for its efforts and why this seems either less or more than it expects. Therefore the economist must concern himself with all those secondary measurements which assist him in judging the profitability of a single enterprise or of a country. Once he admits the need to measure these aggregates or their rates of change he admits the need to concern himself with human behaviour in two senses. There is still the purely quantitative element – the aggregate result of the exercise of individual judgements – which has its own independent significance. An example of this is the proportion which depreciation bears to total costs in all corporations whose capitalisation or annual profits fall within certain limits. But there is also a human element which he can no longer legitimately ignore if he is seeking to explain the functioning of the industrial system in a given historical environment. Still less can he ignore it if he is seeking to predict its functioning in an environment which seldom changes very rapidly.

In the traditional theory of the firm the economist has set out to describe the economic limitations within which it must operate and has endeavoured to explain by reference to a rather arbitrary set of motivations why the entrepreneur behaves as he does. He assumes the operation of universal economic laws, or at least he assumes that the entrepreneur is always constrained or prodded by these laws and by these laws alone, even if the entrepreneur is unaware of their existence. He infers that the experienced executive is the man who intuitively achieves the equal marginal productivity of all factors of production and thereby maximises revenue or profit, over as long as possible a period of time. Knowing that the real world exhibits startling digressions from this norm of rational behaviour, and that certain institutional conditions enable the enterprise which has developed some degree of monopoly to act in an irrational or non-logical manner, or in a manner at least inconsistent with the original theories of competitive equilibrium, he has developed his theories, and twisted his curves to cope with these imperfections as they manifest themselves in the economies with which he is familiar. He endeavours to fit each successive complication into some scheme of rational and predictable behaviour. From time to time, however, the load of imperfections becomes somewhat heavy and a climacteric faulting of the theoretical crust takes place. Beyond a certain point no theoretical stystem can survive the burden of modification which it is expected to carry.

If a strong case had been made for the universal validity of the laws on which the existing analysis of the economic behaviour of groups or organisations is based, if the economist could be satisfied that there were very few exceptions to the rules of economic behaviour which he has evolved and that the theory was capable of dealing with an endless series of exceptions, then it might reasonably be argued that the motivation of behaviour in the industrial environment was none of his business. It could be argued that it follows predictable and measurable patterns that it responds to certain stimuli, the nature of which he is aware in a manner which he has measured in a sufficient number of cases to warrant a description of these phenomena as 'laws' of economic behaviour. It would be somewhat bold to suggest that the present analysis of the economic behaviour of the group can claim immunity from criticism, either on the ground of its applicability within the limits of its own assumptions, or on the grounds that it can be successfully modified and made applicable to an environment which is always changing faster than we can study it.

If the present theoretical structure corresponds with reality only in the limiting sense that its conclusions may be said to represent truisms or common sense then it would seem that there are strong *a priori* grounds for assuming that its foundations are inadequate, and that in an effort to preserve a sufficiently malleable environment for our analytical technique, to keep the number and type of variables within its limits, an apparatus has been developed which at its best can give only a partial explanation. Indeed it sometimes gives a completely incorrect explanation because it does not correctly weight those elements of the problem which come within its scope and ignores others which do not. These other elements may operate with marked consistency and regularity and with a force equal and opposite to those which have been isolated in the mistaken belief that they are the sole determinants of the situation. It is equally possible that they may reinforce the known elements and if this happens in a majority of cases the conclusion is too readily drawn that the economic motive is the most powerful, that it is usually sufficiently powerful to override all other motives, and that where it is not sufficiently powerful the other motives may be brought within the scope of economic analysis by the simple process of giving them an economic value.

An excellent example of this may be found in the textbook discussions on mobility of labour, which invariably assume that every man has his price in the sense that a sufficiently high wage will always induce him to move. This may be true, but in the vast majority of cases the additional wage or salary which would have to be paid to induce a man to move is far greater than anything which he is likely to be offered. Therefore the theory, though possibly true in the limiting exceptional sense to which the economist is so partial, is not only inadequate as an explanation of immobility but a positive hindrance to accurate thought on the problem. An adequate theory must surely provide a complete explanation of the behaviour under consideration. It would have to consider all the motives which operate on the average employee under various circumstances and would provide a technique for evaluating their relative strength, even if this could not be done in terms of pounds and pence. Our present theory is quite incapable of explaining, except by the use of the word 'friction', the fact that different rates of pay for the same work have for generations been paid in towns less than forty miles apart. The fact that there has been some small movement from the one town to the other, in the case which I have in mind, is an indication not of the weakness of the economic motive but of the great strength of the other forces inhibiting purely 'economic' behaviour.

This is a minor example in a field which does not feature prominently in the history of Rolls-Royce, but there is nevertheless ample evidence to confirm this analysis. The remainder of this chapter discusses some of the more important ground upon which the claim is based, that some of the accepted rationalisations of the behaviour of the entrepreneur should be treated with some scepticism. My purpose is to illustrate the overall complexity and the frequently irrational nature of the decision-making process.

Rolls-Royce has not been, and is not, an exceptional firm in the economic sense. There have been no exceptional factors in its growth, apart from the most important influence of personality, which cannot be found elsewhere. Its unique development and achievement is to a very large degree both a reflection and a result of the outstanding personal qualities of its leaders. Personality is the most unpredictable, and by far the most important single factor in the economic history of this, or any other, enterprise.

The decision which the entrepreneur or his policy committees have to make may, broadly speaking, be classified as follows: technical, production, financial, commercial and general policy. These are areas of decision in which certain elements predominate sufficiently often to warrant classification. The administrative divisions of the organisation usually correspond with these areas of decision and relatively specialised administrative machinery has usually evolved to execute these decisions once made. The general policy decisions are normally made by the executive heads of the organisation independently of their departmental responsibilities and are subject to review by a board of directors whose authority is generally little more than that of a constitutional monarch.

Technical decisions are considered first. The nature of the technique in this particular case is that of the internal combustion engine, and more recently, the jet engine and the diesel engine. The firm is concerned with general automobile engineering technique, since it builds complete cars, but it is not concerned, apart from the general responsibilities of installation, with aeronautical engineering technique, since it does not build aircraft. The automobile field, both from the metallurgical and the general engineering point of view, became relatively stable in the middle thirties. The aeronautical field has never been stable for long and is subject to rapid and unpredictable change.

In an engineering firm such as Rolls-Royce, if the technique is relatively stable, the technical element does not play an important part in policy which concerns itself with the other general aspects of finance, production and sales. If the technical field is unstable however, then general policy considerations become almost entirely and continuously technical in character. This may happen as a result of technical work elsehwere, in other firms or other countries. It may also happen, as is quite often the case in Rolls-Royce, as a result of the firm's experimental work. This was particularly true of the aero division, but less marked in the chassis division.

The definitions of monopoly bears on this problem. A distinction should be made between the type of monopoly which is derived from controlling a whole industry, or some strategic economic factor in an industry or some new technical process or patented component, and the type of monopoly – economic security is probably a more accurate definition – which is derived from the legacy of prestige obtained from earlier technical achievement and the goodwill of governments and the public which this has created. This tends to survive long after the situation which first gave rise to it, mainly because of market conservatism and the bias of experts. Unless all the productive units come under one authority the second type of monopoly can never be complete and is never secure. It cannot necessarily be bought by the expenditure of vast sums on research because technical originality is both rare and capricious.

From time to time some firm in the industry makes an advance which the others have not made. Usually this is a refinement, sometimes it is a revolution, in technique. It is a point of general interest that Rolls-Royce attributes its success to a policy of seeking refinement rather than revolution. The firm has always believed in exploiting its existing designs to the full rather than expending its resources on the realisation of the ideal. Only when the possibilities of refinement are exhausted and everyone has, as it were, caught up, does it become necessary to pursue the ideal.

The achievement of general or partial technical superiority in some direction is the major aim of policy in the industry. If it is achieved the economic factors may up to a point be neglected. If it is not achieved attention to the economic factors will provide no solution and the most efficient production of an obsolete article will not ensure survival. The nature of competitive advantage in such an industry is thus exceedingly complex. There is always a buyer's market in technical quality though the nature of this market in the aircraft industry is different from that in the automobile industry. In the former case there is, in Great Britain, a strong element of monopsony, and both the maintenance and the increase of a firm's share in the market is primarily a technical problem. Costs simply do not enter into the picture, because if a firm has an inferior product the volume of orders will fall and the problem of efficient production will be very great. If it has a technically superior product the volume of orders will be relatively large, the customer has no alternative but to pay the price and the problem of efficient production will be correspondingly small. The economic significance of this state of affairs is dependent on the rate of technical change, the rate of obsolescence of existing equipment – there being no necessary inverse correlation between these two factors – and the mobility of technique within the industry. Nationalisation of the industry, and therefore of research, particularly if there was any general pooling of research facilities – something which is usually claimed as desirable – would remove the principal stimulus to technical innovation; for by removing commercial competition, which is unimportant, it would destroy technical competition, which is of supreme importance.[2]

In the automobile industry the customer is not usually technically expert, nor must he have the best. He is also, being an individual, much more price-conscious. The principle may nevertheless be applied in a more qualified manner. Technical monopoly, and with it great economic advantage for a certain length of time, may be achieved by outstanding innovations which are obviously of universal application. Synchromesh gears, independent suspension and safety glass are examples of innovations eventually adopted by the whole industry. In this industry even Rolls-Royce, a firm with a traditional and accepted excuse for high prices, has had to consider cost in the search for perfection and durability. The customer may always opt for a lower standard if the alternative is beyond his price range. When a government or civil airline buys engines it is interested in several factors, all of them technical, but having some economic bearing on its decision. These are:

(1) The total power available under various conditions.
(2) The weight per unit of power developed.
(3) The bulk (mainly frontal area) per unit of power.
(4) Fuel consumption per hour under various operating conditions.

(5) The maintenance profile.
(6) The cost of overhaul and spares (proved or estimated).
(7) The proved or potential reliability of the engine.
(8) Ease of installation, maintenance and interchangeability.
(9) The parent firm's reputation for follow-up and technical support.
(10) The price of the engine.

Apart from prototype contracts an airline or government never buys one engine and is interested not only in the purchase price, but in the running and capital costs over the entire useful life of the engine. The former may amount to one or two thousand pounds. The latter will amount to twenty or thirty thousand. (These figures were realistic when written. For 'thousands', in 1978, read 'millions', a sad commentary on the ravages of inflation in post-war Britain.) It is the function of the salesman to proclaim, and of the technician to achieve, some degree of technical advantage in one or all of these fields.

The important point for the economist is this. When the properties of a complex product are technically fluid, price competition as such is of negligible importance. Only when the properties are stable do the competitive aspects become economic in character. The customer is of course expert, or has the benefit of expert opinion, and he will invariably buy the engine which is technically and economically most suitable for his purpose. To this conclusion however a rider must be added. It would appear that where the position is relatively stable for any length of time, where no engine has a clear advantage on any or all of the points enumerated above, then the outcome tends to depend largely on the personality of the buyers and sellers, on the past reputation of the various firms, on the personal influence which the seller's experts can exert over the buyer's experts and on numerous other quite irrational factors. When the experts are evenly divided on the question of technical merit, cost and price are occasionally able, like the vacuum-cleaner salesman, to jam their feet in the front door and do some fast talking.

The history of Rolls-Royce provides much evidence in support of the argument that the competence and independence of technical or expert judgement in its own field is greatly overrated. There is a feeling amongst technicians and scientists that in their own fields the criteria of judgement are clearly defined, if not absolute, and that there is little possibility of a wrong technical decision. Only politicians and economists, in their view, conduct fruitless arguments and make decisions which are influenced by oratory rather than facts and logic. This opinion seems to be quite widely held, even amongst those whom its converse so severely censures. The minutes of hundreds of technical discussions, and the memoranda appertaining thereto, show that the non-technical have no grounds for sustaining such a methodological inferiority complex. The really important decisions, and many of the less important, are the occasion of intense controversy and cannot be resolved by an appeal to purely technical criteria. The unknowns are too many, and the decision results from the interplay of knowledge, intuition, personality and the status within the organisation of the individual who is finally responsible for the executive decision.

The truth of this assertion may be judged from the arguments about whether or not the company should produce a 6, 8 or 12-cylinder car, whether it should continue two-stroke engine development or abandon work which had cost hundreds of thousands, whether it should develop contra-flow or axial-flow jet engines. Royce once rejected outright a proposal to employ a proprietary carburettor whose advocate claimed that it was 45 per cent better than the old. He would not have minded in the least, and would probably have investigated the article, had the claim been made that it was 50 or 100 per cent better. The experienced executive has an intense suspicion of bogus precision, especially when applied to major policy decisions.

When the decision is basically technical, but involves economic and administrative elements as well, the number of variables immediately becomes far too large to be handled by any routine system of judgement. A large number of considerations will be raised by the protagonists and antagonists of a particular scheme. These will be graded in order of importance which will differ for each individual according to his profession, training, experience and seniority in the organisation. The number of factors taken into consideration will often bear a high proportion to the numbers of those which, in the event, actually determine the outcome of the policy adopted. The more limited the decision, in the sense of its impact on the formal and informal organisation of the firm, and in the sense of its width (i.e. the number of types of technical knowledge which it involves) the more accurate is the judgement of the individual or committee likely to be. Where technical, economic and general policy factors are combined, the decision is reached by a process of intuitive judgement. In the operation of this process the economic factors are often mere appendages of technical prejudices. An excellent example of this is the unanimous, almost indignant rejection by the board of the proposal made by C. S. Rolls just before his death in 1911, that the company should manufacture the Wright aero-engines. This would have given Rolls-Royce a very considerable advantage but the proposal was rejected on the grounds that the idea was more suitable for an H. G. Wells novel than for adoption by a serious-minded engineering firm.

This evidence is not intended to suggest that all technical decisions are arbitrary, or that they are determined solely by chance or personality, merely that the limits of decision within which the influence of personality is the most important factor vary widely according to the scope of the decision. It does not necessarily imply that the limits are always very wide for the complex general policy decisions, or very narrow for the very confined decisions within a technical subdivision, since in many cases there is frequenty a dominant limiting factor which immediately makes its appearance. The project costs too much, some other firm is too far advanced on similar work, or the technical capacity of some department cannot be further expanded. It is difficult to resist the conclusion that in the field of general policy decision in which the economist is most interested, his generalisations have often been somewhat facile and naive.

In the sphere of production policy, much the same conclusion obtains. When considering production policy management is usually faced with a given historical situation. It has so much capital, limited technical and administrative capacity, so many employees, a certain size of factory, a market whose general characteristics are known. It is not often that the entrepreneur 'goes into business' afresh, either in a new factory or a new product, or in a new scale of production for an old product. When he does so, and Rolls-Royce has certainly done so in all senses, the calculations are often most rudimentary. One calculation of production costs for a shadow factory gave a higher cost of producing 400 engines per month than for 200 engines per month. In each case the totals were simply the result of adding detailed estimates for various items of cost. There was no evident consciousness of conflict between this conclusion and economic law or common sense though the management was by no means unacquainted with the fact or ignorant of the broad theory of economies of scale. There is invariably an allowance for contingencies of from 10 to 20 per cent (which in this case represented a capital sum of £600,000) and from this some of that school of thinkers who advocate planning industrial production on a national scale might conclude that the management of this firm is either incompetent or inefficient or both. They might even conclude that, even if they are efficient, they achieve the right results in the wrong way. Such a conclusion is not justified. The entrepreneur does not attempt to make these calculations of marginal advantage and disadvantage, except in the broadest sense, because he realises that they will not have any effect on the success of the project in hand. The decision to build or not to build, to expand or to contract, to enter a new field or to stay out, does not depend on the rate of interest, it does not depend on rising or falling wage rates, it does not depend on whether a crankcase can be built for £20.34 if the factory makes 200 a month and £24.43 if it makes 100 a month. It depends on the assessment of innumerable factors which cannot be given a monetary equivalent as well as on those which can. It depends on whether the firm has, or can get the necessary capital, and if it can get it the management is not concerned, within reasonable limits, with what it costs. It depends on technical and administrative capacity, always the most important limitation where expansion is concerned, on the supply of genuinely skilled labour, on the assessment of the market for the new product or additional output and on a whole composite of factors which even the detailed history of a particular scheme cannot hope wholly to describe.

There seems to be an air of inevitability about these major policy decisions which is difficult to analyse. They are either inevitable and have to be taken, or they are not inevitable and are not taken.[3]

It seems legitimate to conclude that unless there is a very heavy balance of advantage in favour of a major decision – and the assessment of this advantage is intuitive rather than rational – it will not be taken. In the situations which an examination of the board minutes and policy documents covering some forty years of every phase of this company's activity have brought to light, the rate of interest and the movement of wages rates have never once been considered in the process of reaching major policy decisions. The significance of this may be left to others to explore.

At the other extreme there are the routine policy decisions concerning production which is already being carried out on a certain scale. In this connection it is important to bear in mind the fact that Rolls-Royce have always produced small quantities. This has been a deliberate policy, although the management has often contemplated a digression into the quantity production field. They regard as quantity production a figure of 10,000 vehicles per annum or over. The management has always been conscious of the rather exclusive nature of the chassis market for which their product is designed. They did not consciously set out to achieve this reputation of quality, but their policy did achieve it, and it is a difficult reputation to uphold. Despite the increasing technical and economic problems involved in maintaining the pre-eminence of the chassis, the company would rather have suffered, and in fact did suffer, a loss than allow this reputation to fade. There is a commercial element in this because, despite the volume of aero-engine business the goodwill value of the name is still largely associated with the production of cars. But there is also an obstinate element of technical pride, a feeling that superlative engineering quality still has its merits even if the State thinks it necessary, for reasons of social policy, to eliminate entirely the incomes which are necessary to maintain the market. The company continued to manufacture cars in the late thirties when the logical, rational thing to do was to cease manufacture. The company continued to manufacture because the individuals concerned would have been quite genuinely ashamed to advocate such a policy.

Because of the peculiar nature of its market the management has never had much trouble in deciding on output. Past experience has been a reliable constant, and the works have never committed themselves to long runs, ordering large batches of material, or producing well ahead of sales requirements. Until 1936 the car was never designed from a production point of view and consequently the quantity aspects of production did not present many problems for decision. Where materials and proprietary components were concerned the management was conscious of the advantage of buying large quantities, but quality always won the day over cost.

The other important spheres of decision in production concern the proportion of the product manufactured in the works, the methods of manufacture, and costs of production. Decisions on manufacturing methods have an important bearing on, and are sometimes influenced by costs. Under other circumstances, of which a good example will be given later, the problem of cost is paramount. It is impossible however to separate these three completely, because the problems do not exist separately. The history of Rolls-Royce provides no example of a decision, even when the company was particularly concerned with the cost problem, which might be described as a deliberate and conscious effort to reach the lowest point on the average cost curve, either for the component or for the entire vehicle, by varying the quantity alone.

The decisions during the First World War, for example, to take advantage of the large sub-contract organisation which has been created in the United States for the manufacture of Eagle aero-engine parts and to produce cars in that country, is of outstanding interest because they were taken on the basis of a rational calculation of economic advantage and possibility. It is the only decision which would please the economic purist, and though it does not necessarily follow that this is why the project failed disastrously, it is significant that it did fail disastrously. It failed because too little attention was paid to the non-economic factors in the situation, which some sceptical businessmen appreciated at the outset but which they were unable to formulate precisely. It failed because the current attitudes of the policy-makers, their standards of correct and proper conduct, both technical and economic, were too rigidly entrenched for them to be convinced of the need for flexibility and change.

The project was entered on both sides in a mood of high optimism since the economic logic was very compelling. Experienced Rolls-Royce engineers, with a wide knowledge of American resources and Rolls-Royce manufacturing methods, were already in America. The American people were car-minded, the Rolls-Royce name had great prestige, and the size of the upper income groups was greater than in any other country. The English management were suspicious of industrial and social conditions in Europe and was anxious to spread its activities beyond the United Kingdom. The American company was starting from scratch but with all the experience of Derby behind it.

All these factors were considered and it was thought that the project 'could not fail'. But both costs and sales were grossly overestimated. The American company laboured from the start under a financial burden which it could not support and the English company lost the American market for ten years.

The causes of this failure may be found in two principal categories, the non-economic factors which were neglected or ignored by the management, and the general attitudes prevailing, particularly at Derby, which undermined the confidence and responsibility of the local management and allowed the enthusiasm of the American backers to be replaced by disillusion and distrust.

The first of the neglected factors was the American sense of values, and of value. It was assumed as almost axiomatic that if there were 20,000 rich men in the United States and 5000 in England the sales would be at least in the proportion of 4:1 though it is noteworthy that this judgement was not backed to the extent of erecting a production plant capable of fulfilling this demand. Such an estimate ignored the characteristics of the rich American, whose sales resistance to the American Rolls-Royce car derived from two important attitudes. In the first place he was less susceptible, through the mere fact of his wealth, to that type of social pleasure which in other countries force all rich people to behave as rich people do, even when this overrides their sense of value for money. In the second place, as one American millionaire himself remarked, the average wealthy American 'felt a pretentious ass' in a Rolls-Royce car. A third factor was the large number of equivalent American vehicles at a quarter the price, there being insufficient logic to explain the advantage to be derived from the other three-quarters. A market characteristic which was neglected was the trade-in system, which in England had been considered beneath the dignity of Rolls-Royce distributors. Unfortunately what was 'not done' in England was 'done' in America, and the policy had to be abandoned. It was then discovered that handling trade-in business on such a small scale was most unprofitable and added to the overheads which had to be recovered on the sale of new cars. A further disappointment was the price which was obtainable for a second-hand Rolls-Royce in the United States. For some strange, and to the English management quite illogical reason, it was considered to be worth about one-sixth of the value of an equivalent car in England.

These were the main factors neglected in the market. On the side of production policy some equally grave mistakes were made, most of them the result of decisions taken in England by men who visualised the problems in terms of English conditions, and whose attitudes were dominated by a group of rather important prejudices. The first of these was that the Americans could not produce a quality car. The second was that quality and quantity were two quite irreconcilable objectives. The third arose from a deep-seated fear that the American management would get out of control, come under the influence of American mass-production ideas and produce a Rolls-Royce completely different from that produced in England. It was felt, and no one ever thought it necessary to give a convincing explanation of this attitude, that this would be quite intolerable. This prejudice was happily rationalised as the road to disaster for both companies. And at the very highest level, owing to the somewhat tenuous nature of the voting exercised from England, there was constant preoccupation with the effect on the English company's future of what was happening at Springfield. Loss of control was a fear always uppermost in the minds of the English management.

The policy laid down by Derby that the Springfield management should adhere rigidly to a policy of complete identity of product was too conservative and impractical to last long and it was abandoned piecemeal under the pressure of continual and embittered controversy. The strength of the economic argument was overwhelmingly great, since a Rolls-Royce electrical system would have cost 424 dollars to produce compared with 115 dollars for a high-quality local product. There were also absurd technical anomalies, the first cars being produced with petrol tank fillers which were too small for American pumps. Such things were changed, but the essential principle remained and was consistently applied for several years.

A second policy which was incorporated in the original agreement between the parent and its subsidiary was that the American company should always produce the same model as the English company. If Derby brought out a new mark of vehicle, Springfield was obliged to follow suit almost immediately. The argument which supported this policy was that all sales in America would cease if it was once thought that the American chassis was out-of-date. Several junior executives who visited America stressed the futility of these policies, but they were regarded as inexperienced and their views were ignored.

The financial relations between the two firms were equally bedevilled by pride and prejudice. The English management was loath to contribute financial assistance in any shape or form and they came to regard the American financiers as grasping capitalists whose sole interest in the project was financial. This was not the case; and the attitude created an equal and opposite resentment amongst the bankers, some of whom had made very great efforts to salvage the American company. They were unable to secure technical control and in their despair endeavoured at one stage to buy control of the English company.

Between these two poles of opposition the local management failed to formulate or apply an effective policy. Such a policy would naturally have aimed at producing a product which would have secured the identical reputation in the hands of the customer. It would have taken full advantage of American productive methods and of the existing organisation of the American motor industry. It would have sought the maximum quality consistent with the production of a quantity sufficiently large to ensure a reasonable distribution of overheads. It would have produced a car at a price which did not grossly offend the American sense of value for money.

It is of course easy to see all this looking backwards, but the accounts and cost figures of the company alone do not tell this story, and it is significant that when the great danger of the situation was finally appreciated the local management became preoccupied with the most careful analysis of various cost and production possibilities. These elaborate calculations pointed to two simple facts. The cars cost too much and they were not wanted. The situation in its totality had been misjudged and only a complete re-formation of policy based on a reassessment of the whole situation would have enabled the American company to continue. It did not have, and could not obtain at any price, the finance to do so. Success it seems, succeeds, failure fails. From this episode the conclusion may be drawn that it is far better to get all the elements partly right than to get some wholly right and others wholly wrong. Success does not depend on the lore of nicely calculated less or more by itself. Nor can the economist explain success or failure in terms of this lore.

The second example has been chosen because the elements of the thinking which it has involved will be especially familiar to the economist. It also illustrates, incidentally, the point just made that the entrepreneur and his staff become very economically minded when things begin to go wrong and start elaborate witch-hunts of a more general character. It also illustrates the contention that these calculations never solve the problem and that the most useful men that a firm possesses are those who can visualise the problem in its totality, who can ask the right questions and examine critically the strategic economic objectives of the organisation.

In this case the deficiency of policy was an established tradition of the firm, a series of almost instinctive beliefs inherited from Sir Henry Royce. They were the following:

(1) That there would always be a market for superlative quality in automobile engineering;
(2) That Rolls-Royce would emasculate its goodwill by producing in quantity since quantity and quality were incompatible;
(3) That even if this were not so the customer thought so and he was always right;
(4) Selling a few hundred costly cars had always paid;
(5) An inferior component, however cheap, was never justified if something better could be produced, however costly;

(6) Rolls-Royce would antagonise the industry by entering the quantity market;

(7) Derby was unfamiliar with quantity production and it would be costly to breed this familiarity.

Before 1935 economic circumstances had made it possible for these cherished beliefs to become strongly established although from time to time, beginning as far back as 1913, far-sighted individuals had been doubtful about some or all of these tenets which comprised the 'tradition' of the firm. In this year the chassis division made a loss and it continued to be unprofitable until the outbreak of war. This was attributed primarily to high costs of production, but since very little attention had ever been paid to cost it was decided to investigate the problem. This investigation showed that high cost could be blamed on the following factors:

(1) The small number of cars produced;
(2) The large variety of types having hardly any common parts;
(3) The cost of high-quality components specially manufactured to Rolls-Royce standards;
(4) Small-quantity purchasing of materials and components;
(5) The high cost of coach-built bodies which supplied little more than individuality;
(6) The complications of Bentley and Rolls-Royce design.

Comparisons with the cost breakdowns of other vehicles revealed all these features. They also revealed that by far the most important factor was the size of the overhead which had to be spread over 1000 cars. To achieve the target price of £950 and absorb the overhead meant a reduction in chassis manufacturing costs of about £300. By approximately quadrupling the quantity produced this figure could easily have been reached, but this idea could not be entertained, and the problem had to be solved the hard way. It was found that for many of the bought-out components, significant reductions could be achieved in the unit cost by employing dies and tools. But such dies and tools were expensive and this expense could only be warranted by quantity production. A further reduction could be achieved by buying out electrical components, carburettors and other items such as propellor-shafts from the specialist manufacturer who supplied the whole industry. There was some move in this direction after much discussion but the overall effect was slight in the industrial world (pure logic keeps very strange company).

A further interesting example of business psychology is supplied by the conflict with manufacturers' price rings which existed amongst the chassis-frame and alloy steel manufacturers. It was found that both Rolls-Royce and Rovers were paying 10d a pound for crankshaft forgings which could have been produced for 4d. This was considered so outrageous that the erection of an independent foundry was contemplated, but the quantity which would have had to be produced was too large and the project was abandoned. One manufacturer outside the ring did quote a very much lower figure, but this was not adopted. 'It is necessary', said the chief chassis engineer, 'to keep within the Alloy Steel Association as outside this I cannot find a firm upon whose experience and good faith I could rely.' Nor would an order be given where the quotation was known to be below cost. For some reason it was considered to be unwise to do so.

After several years of work on this problem one of the responsible officials concluded: 'we are only beginning to learn the art of purchasing at competitive prices.' The use of the word 'art' in this context is significant because it so effectively describes an attitude of mind.

The main result of this elaborate investigation was the evolution of a project to rationalise chassis production by commonising and simplifying components on the 'Meccano' principle. This was the best that could be done if the board would not contemplate quantity production. It enabled the same quantity, and if anything a larger number of projected types, to be made with greater economy of effort, particularly on the experimental side, and was a logical step. It was not put into practice until after the war, but it enabled the relative price increase of Rolls-Royce products to be kept lower than any other car in the industry.

Yet it is quite clear that this investigation revealed four factors which the management preferred to disregard, because the overall change of policy which their recognition required was as substantial as its execution would have been difficult and inconvenient, especially during rearmament. These factors were the following:

(1) The U.S.A. had succeeded in mass-producing quality, if not exclusiveness, in the comparable class of vehicle, at a fifth of the cost. This was openly admitted within the organisation.
(2) The redistribution of incomes in the United Kingdom was seriously diminishing the size of the upper-income groups, who were becoming more price-conscious.

(3) The stabilisation in the design of the automobile meant that technical innovation had become more costly and that in consequence no firm could afford the experimental establishment necessary to keep far ahead in all fields of engineering.

(4) The margin of quality which the firm could offer for the price which it had to ask was small and diminishing steadily.

The chassis division was obviously living on its name and a complete reorientation of policy was necessary. It was advocated by several people but until the outbreak of war there was no sign of its evolution.

This is an example of the conflict of economic logic with technical and commercial tradition, of the unwillingness of the management to answer the difficult but pertinent question put to them by a senior designer in 1935: 'Are we to forsake quality for quantity or find some outlet for our energies where quality can be made to pay?' The question was framed in the form of a false antithesis, but it suggested that the only genuine solution would required a change of policy.

These two examples show clearly that the entrepreneur's theories, dogmas and attitudes cannot be ignored as major determinants of the economic problem. The most influential segment of these beliefs, which in due course develop into the traditions of an organisation, comprises those norms of conduct and behaviour, of profitability and distribution, which he has come to regard as either average or ideal. Whether the average is considered to be just, or just to be average, is an important point. In all social organisations – and the industrial unit is probably the most important and the least studied organisation in human society – there exist, and if they do not exist they will soon be created, standards of behaviour which govern the functions and performance of its members. The moral law or, if we prefer another term, the social pressure which supports these norms of conduct, is stronger than is generally realised, and if economic or any other incentives run counter to a widely held and long-established concept of 'reasonable' behaviour, however illogical such behaviour may be under changed circumstances, there is little doubt which influence will prevail.

What, then, determines the general character of the policy-making activity of the executive staff? The problem may be conceived in terms of the immediacy of impact of concentric circles of the environment, all interdependent, never stable, each outer circle obscured from the view of the man at the centre by mountain ranges of strongly held expert opinion, of prejudice and bias and of the historical attitudes of the social organisation which supports and is supported by industrial activity.

The immediate inner circles of the environment always demands the most attention and in it is included the day-to-day administration in all departments. Habit, precedent and routine can usually handle all these decisions. This is essential because the capacity to handle novel decisions is always limited. The second circle of the environment can best be described as the sphere of internal policy. The decisions in this sphere are invariably marginal in character – to increase or diminish output, the proportion of components bought out, the expenditure on welfare, dividends, or a particular project of research, to alter the distribution of existing production facilities or of productive effort. This type of decision is usually handled inter-departmentally since it embraces several spheres of activity. The general proportions and relevant factors in such decisions can usually be perceived by all the participants to some degree.

The two outer circles in the environment of decision embrace those areas in which the novel elements predominate. The first is the general policy decision, which may be classed as an attempt by the organisation to influence or control some aspect of the environment in which it has to operate. The adoption of a new product, of new methods of production or the extension of operations vertically or horizontally in an effort to seek competitive efficiency or independence from outside sources of supply should be included in this category of decision. The final circle comprises the general policy decision which results from independent changes in the environment which the organisation may or may not have anticipated, and over which it has little control. The greater the anticipation the greater the control which the organisation will possess over the impact of such changes.

These are obviously not rigid distinctions and the complexity of the interdependence of different types of decision is clearly the dominant feature of the problem. Like all generalisations they are valuable provided too much is not expected of them. It is probably unnecessary to emphasise that the average executive is concerned with all four spheres of decision at once. The successful executive is the man who looks inwards and outwards, forwards and backwards at the same time. In this, as in other spheres, leadership consists in the power to comprehend the whole, to derive a policy which is applicable to the whole and not only to a part of the problem, and to apply it vigorously.

The strategy and tactics of industrial and military operations are not dissimilar.

The dominant factor in the decision-making process in the inner circles is the informal organisation of the structure, the general pattern of human relationships which is created by a particular activity and which must usually be changed if the nature or intensity of this activity is to change. The dominant factor in the outer circles of general policy decisions is the degree of knowledge of the situation and of the variables which affect it; the decision may not appear to be rational if considered in terms of the known elements, but it is usually rational to the extent that the known elements are properly weighted against the unknowns. The objective of all policy is the survival of the organisation as a social institution.

The use of the word social rather than economic is deliberate, because it seems that whether or not the entrepreneur is conscious of the fact he pays attention to the economic factor only in so far as it forces itself upon his attention, and the force of this factor varies greatly from firm to firm. It also varies greatly between firms whose general circumstances the economist would normally regard as similar, if not identical, and it varied greatly in its impact on the same firm from one period to another.

It may therefore be argued with some conviction that the complexity and interdependence of the factors involved has been conveniently disregarded, the importance of personality and tradition has been grossly underestimated and, because profit is the most visible index of industrial efficiency, the economist has been content to construct his theories on the basis of the plausible assumption that a symptom of industrial health is the principal regulator of industrial activity. He has also assumed into the process of decision far more logic and uniformity than is warranted, except in the case of the simplest decisions.

It may be suggested that this conclusion can only apply to the particular firm which has generously provided the raw material for this study, but the analysis would apply equally to Bristols, De Havillands, Napiers and Armstrong-Siddeleys. It would apply in some degree to the entire aircraft industry, and to a lesser degree to all firms. R. G. Collingwood has provided an illuminating analysis of the maxim 'know thyself'. It means, he says, 'knowing first, what it is to be a man, secondly, knowing what it is to be the kind of man you are, and thirdly, knowing what it is to be the kind of man you are and nobody else is'. In studying an industrial enterprise one becomes acutely conscious that it is (a) Rolls-Royce, (b) a firm in the engineering industry, (c) a firm – a type of human organisation engaging in productive activity. The weakness of the present analytical apparatus is that it is preoccupied with (c) is hardly aware of (b) and has never heard of (a). If the problem is approached in the reverse order – the proper study of mankind being man, not men – the generalisations made so confidently under (c) will have a far greater realism and relevance than they at present possess.

In conclusion it may be asked what relevance, if any, this discussion has to the general character of economic thought. The following conclusions are suggested rather tentatively, more as a basis of discussion than as a new nihilistic dogma. Firstly, how widely are these conclusions as to the general subservience of the economic motive applicable? It is the present writer's opinion that they extend beyond the theory of the firm, which will require in due course, as more studies of particular firms are made, not only revision but complete reconstruction. (Since the above was written there has, of course, been a much wider study of industrial organisations, not least by economists, but we have merely scratched the surface and old attitudes die hard, especially in old professions!)

Too many conclusions have been drawn from too few facts and the pure gold of the economic motive has been refined far beyond the point that the social metallurgist would consider profitable. In the alloy of human behaviour the economic motive may be as significant as the carbon content of steel, but a more adequate understanding of human behaviour requires some knowledge of iron as well as carbon. A new set of questions needs to be devised and a great many more empirical studies of human behaviour in industry and commerce must be undertaken if they are to be answered with any degree of satisfaction.

This is not intended to imply that the economic problem has disappeared, still less that it has ceased to be economic. There will always be methods of employing resources which are more efficient than other methods. And it is more necessary today than it has ever been to study these differences and to elucidate the principles which underlie them. They will probably not suffer any great alteration if more attention is paid to the human motivations upon which the operation of the industrial system depends. The hard core of economic logic will not be eliminated by newfangled science and economic analysis will continue to suggest means whereby the fortresses of poverty and inefficiency may be assaulted. But it will do so more effectively if it ceases to be intrigued by the ingenuity of its own refinements and if it ceases to seek in the perversity of reality an excuse for profitless speculation as to what the entrepreneur will do or should do under a set of circumstances which are entirely economic in character. Emmet's cartoons are amusing, but they will not help us to build railways.

It is never presumptuous to suggest that any field of thought, and the methods which it employs, might benefit from a comparison with the general characteristics of philosophical thought in the classical age of Greece. Though there are few who can suggest without presumption that they are competent to carry out such a comparison, T. S. Eliot, in this categorical age of the atomic bomb, might be accepted as one of the few who would escape such a charge. In his 'Notes Towards a Definition of Culture' he has risked a generalisation which is not without relevance to the problems under discussion here:

> The advantage of the study of Greek history and Greek political theory, as a preliminary to the study of other history and other theory, is its manageability. It has to do with a small area, with men rather than with masses, and with human passions of individuals rather than with those vast impersonal forces which in our modern society are a necessary convenience of thought, and the study of which tends to obscure the study of the human being.

No body of knowledge in the social sciences is more secure than the knowledge of human behaviour upon which it is based, and it is for this reason that the suggestion is made above that we re-examine the foundations when the cracks in the structure appear even faster than the writing on the wall. Thought, like other organisations, has pronounced bureaucratic tendencies. Few would deny that our civilisation is in greater need today than ever before of thought which has relevance for the solution of practical problems. Such thought is not any the less worthy on this account, nor is the objective of securing the survival of our civilisation one which the academic mind should spurn. If therefore, as all the available evidence seems to suggest, the human problem in industry is of paramount importance, it is surely the duty of those who regard themselves as social scientists to confer on this problem the patronage of their study and thought.

Notes

CHAPTER 2

1. From Colonel Darby's minute of his discussion with Monsieur Dollfuss.
2. This term is used here to imply the benefit which the company might obtain from employing its best technicians in other directions.
3. The prices quoted per engine were:

Up to 100	£3300
Up to 200	£3200
300 and over	£3100

4. The Ford engineers made a very thorough study of the Merlin, which they criticised on four grounds:
    (1) The gears were not true involutes and therefore required special finishing.
    (2) The supercharger drive was most complicated and its manufacture called for a high degree of workmanship.
    (3) It was considered that the engine could use a cast crankshaft 'with enormous saving in machining time due to ability to cast close to finished size'. The speed of the shaft was low compared with car work and the stresses moderate.
    (4) It was not proposed to do any hand-chamfering or filing. All this was to be machined.
   The problem of gear-production was considered to be the weakest link in the chain of any Merlin production scheme. This criticism was soon borne out by events in England.
5. In a report written on 12 December the two Rolls-Royce representatives at Bordeaux, Willis and Buxton, made the following pertinent observation:
   'This Company in the past, in the production of Ford cars, have had all the construction and organising work done for them by the American parent concern, who have prepared all designs of highly specialised plant and tools and have managed the planning and starting of plant here, leaving only the maintenance work to be done by themselves, with the result that the organisation here do not appear to know how to start on their own initiative without outside help to start the plant for them.'
6. Dollfuss estimated that a further 375 machine tools would have to be provided.

CHAPTER 3

1. Maurice Olley had worked for Rolls-Royce (Inc.) at Springfield, Massachusetts, before the war.

2. These problems are effectively discussed in the Harvard Report on the acceleration of aircraft manufacture in the U.S.A. This pointed out that:
   > Many of the changes in engine and airframe manufacturing processes between 1940 and 1944 could be classed as differences in kind, not just differences in degree. While techniques were borrowed from other industries the special characteristics of airframes and engines made it impossible to adopt the established techniques of any other industry without revisions. To meet wartime production goals the manufacturers of airframes and engines are not just forced to do on a vastly greater scale, a job they had already been doing in peacetime. They had to do an essentially different job which neither they nor others had ever done.

3. A thorough analytical study of the performance of the firm in this respect has not yet been made. It would provide valuable information on the methods and effectiveness of this type of production control, and until it is done no really adequate history of the Second World War can be written, either for the firm or the industry. It would however be a major undertaking in itself, and though the subject will of necessity be discussed at length in the following pages, the strength of any conclusions which are drawn is limited by the somewhat inexact and incomplete nature of the figures available from the firm's records.

4. The small output of repaired engines in the early months of 1940 was responsible for a suggestion that more repairs should be taken away from Derby and given to one of the motor firms to carry out. The Alvis Company and the Clement Talbot Company had already been brought into the scheme. Rolls-Royce believed that only by repairing their own engines could the firm both learn by experience and incorporate the latest modifications in the repaired engines. On 27 February Hives wrote to Freeman and to Sir Kingsley Wood strongly opposing the proposal:
   > We view with alarm any suggestion of reorganising aero-engine repairs. . . . One can argue that dealing with aero-engine repairs requires more expert knowledge than the production of new pieces, and this especially applies in wartime when it is fundamental that the maximum service and efficiency shall be obtained from all engines and materials. If we are going to maintain technical superiority in the air it is essential that those with the expert knowledge shall be allowed to guide the policy.

   In due course, the volume of repair work increased so greatly that further firms had to be brought into the scheme. But the central control was always exercised by Rolls-Royce.

5. Warner and Low, op cit.

6. Alexander M. Leighton, *The Governing of Men: General Principles and Recommendations Based on Experience at a Japanese Relocation Camp* (Princeton University Press, 1946).

CHAPTER 4

1. The author of a well-known and influential *Newsletter* which did much to alert public opinion in the late 1930s to the dangers of Nazism in Germany.
2. There was a substantial repair organisation in existence by June 1940. Merlins were being repaired, and in some cases parts manufactured at the factories of the De Havilland, Alvis, Talbot and Napier Companies, as well as at Derby, Belper, Glasgow and the Manchester Ford works. Hucknall's main function was to provide facilities for handling the great increase in repair work which suddenly took place during the crisis months of 1940.
3. The Hurricane was the first aircraft to receive top priority, on 19 May, followed by the others on 24 May.
4. The reasons for this are fully set out in Professor Schlaifer's remarkable study of aircraft engine development in Great Britain and America. He attributes the lack of American liquid-cooled engines primarily to the absence of an adequate market for these engines in America. The major engine-building firms became interested primarily in air-cooled engines, for which there was a large civil market. (See R. Schlaifer and S. D. Heron, *The Development of Aircraft Engines and Fuels* (Bailey Bros, 1952), Chs X and XI.)
5. This is a commonly accepted fallacy. Mass-production methods involve a high degree of accuracy and Ford production methods were no exception. The mass production of the Merlin by Ford could easily have been achieved, as its eventual mass production by Glasgow and the Packard Company proves. The industrial history of the Second World War demonstrated that the most complex piece of machinery can, if necessary, be produced by mass production methods to the smallest tolerances. What usually suffered was not the accuracy of the finished parts but the rate at which modifications could be introduced. 'Mass', in this context, implies rigidity of production methods.
6. This company itself went into liquidation some years after the war.
7. In his report on the Packard Merlin, Colonel Vincent makes the following comment on his problem:

> While we had the wholehearted co-operation of representatives of the Rolls-Royce Company, there was naturally a wide divergence of opinion as to how important engineering items should be handled. For many months the argument centred around what parts should be made special for British engines and during this time our plans were changed from day to day. We started with the understanding that we were to build the same engine for both governments and ended up with the decision to build engines for the British which were installationally interchangeable with British units. . . . It would be hard to estimate the time that was spent discussing British versus U.S. production, engineering and testing practices, but we should not overlook the fact that all concerned received a liberal education that resulted in a definite benefit to both governments.

8. An interesting comment on the general character of American proficiency in production methods was made in a report of one of the Rolls-Royce representatives to Derby in December 1942.

> Generally speaking, American machining practice and methods are in line with British practice, but where they seem to score is in the planning, organisation and handling of the work, which demands a continuous flow through the line. The best brains are employed during the preparatory planning layout. . . . Machining sections are laid out in model form a quarter of an inch to the foot. On this plan every detail is considered and the final arrangement is based on the estimated time or times for each operation and the minimum amount of effort per operator by introducing features such as automatic clamping, minimum body movement etc. . . . *all with a view to keeping the man in the best physical condition right up to the end of the shift.* (Italics mine.)

9. Items bought out included fuel pumps, boost control, coolant pump, camshaft, valves, clutchplate, bronze bushes, ball and roller bearings, main and connecting-rod bearings, ignition harnesses and miscellaneous small items. In the early stages aluminium castings were also bought out.

10. Late in 1943, when the success of the Packard Merlin had been proved beyond any doubt, the demands for the engine on both sides of the Atlantic increased so heavily that the U.S. authorities seriously considered expanding production facilities beyond the Packard organisation. The Continental Aircraft Corporation (which had manufactured small-horsepower aero-engines before the war) agreed to lay down a Merlin line and preliminary arrangements were made in 1944. The project did not materialise, however, as it became obvious by the middle of 1944 that the additional output would no longer be required.

CHAPTER 5

1. The 40 mm cannon was fitted to a small number of Hurricanes in 1942 and some of these aircraft were employed as tank-busters in North Africa. Hives argued very forcibly in favour of the development of this or a similar combination for anti-tank work but the idea did not meet with a favourable reception. His contention that the tank was most vulnerable to the right type of attack from the air was nevertheless convincingly supported when the armour-piercing rocket projectile was developed.

2. On 27 May 1943 Air Vice-Marshal Sorley (then in charge of research and development at the Air Ministry) wrote to Hives expressing regret at this decision. 'Although the work which you have done for us has not led to the introduction of a Rolls-Royce gun for general service use, I can assure you that your participation in the gun design field has had a most healthy effect upon the older establishments and firms engaged on this type of work.'

3. The Merlin X was similar to the Merlin III (which was almost identical to the Merlin II) except for a different reduction gear ratio and a Farman-type supercharger drive. This had been developed when difficulties were experienced with a more novel type of two-speed supercharger on which

work had been in progress since January 1935. These were the Merlins with which the R.A.F. entered the war.

The next important modification was the introduction of a pressurised cooling system using only 30 per cent glycol, which first appeared in a small number of Merlin IVs and which came into production in September 1939 on the Merlin XII.

The development of superchargers, which had begun when Ellor came over from the R.A.E. in 1927, was greatly intensified when S. G. Hooker joined the company in 1938. Much work was done on the supercharging of a special racing Merlin with which an attempt on the world's speed record had been contemplated. The results of this work were incorporated in the two-speed single-stage supercharger of the Merlin XX which went into production in July 1940, and in the single-speed Merlin XIV which went into production in January 1941 and replaced the Merlin XII in the Spitfire V. For a detailed discussion of the technical history of these projects see Schlaifer, op. cit., pp. 223–30.

4. These reasons were the following. Surplus engines were required to cover:
    1. Engines required in transit to manufacturers and squadrons.
    2. Stocks maintained at squadrons.
    3. The completion of older marks of aircraft which were not adaptable to newer marks of engine which might have come into production before the airframe programme had been completed.
    4. The provision of a stock of engines as an insurance against bombing.
5. Some of the requests for information which were received indicated clearly that the reorganisation at the M.A.P. had left some officials high and dry on islands of paper which were quite isolated from the mainland of the industry. On 27 July more than a year after production had started at Crewe, the following telegram was received from the M.A.P.

'Re Crewe Merlin and Glasgow wire anticipated date completion of buildings and plant and when production partial or otherwise can commence. A.P.E. Air-minded Harrogate.'

This was ignored, though it caused much amusement. It was followed a month later by a further telegram.

'A.P.F. 291 27/8 Wire briefly or write by return if possible progress plant and machine tools, when installation commenced or when expected start. What items holding up installation of balanced unit percentage plant in production. Production labour at work as a percentage total labour required full production. D.A.P.F.6.'

Copies of these telegrams, with the request that the author should be discovered, were sent to R. H. Coverley with Hives' comment: 'We have started a form-filling-in department for the Ministry of Labour, the Ministry of Health and the M.A.P. but Mr D.A.P.F.6 we propose to ignore.'

6. The two-stage supercharger was first tested in April 1941.

CHAPTER 6

1. The existence of an aerodrome at Hucknall again proved a great advantage. The aircraft were flown in, fitted with Merlin XLVs and flown out. The engines were modified in the repair shop at Derby.
2. An August 1940 programme envisaged a production of 1477 in April 1941. The output actually achieved was 721. This was double the figure asked for in a programme issued six months earlier.
3. This figure was calculated on the basis of tools required to increase production from 177 to 300 Merlins per week assuming a 65 per cent utilisation of machines working 130 hours per week on the two-shift system.
4. Statistical comparisons made between the two factories in June 1941 illustrate the effect on efficiency of different production techniques and layouts. Derby machining hours were 53 per cent greater than Glasgow, Crewe machining hours were only 11 per cent greater.

CHAPTER 7

1. The following were the comparative specifications of the Meteor and the Liberty at this time:

	Meteor	*Liberty*
Weight	1450	1350
Horsepower	550	340
Lbs/h.p.	2.64	3.98
Height	31″	24.5″
Length	49.5″	61.25″
Width	30.25″	28.0″

The horsepower estimate for the Meteor was conservative.

2. It was held in some quarters that the Meteor engine was essentially an aero-engine and *therefore* not suitable for tanks. The engine was obviously not designed as a tank-engine but the question of its suitability in this case turned on whether or not it could be easily and effectively modified. Modification presented some problems but none of these were insoluble and none of these objections were capable of outweighing the blatant reality of the fact that no other suitable high-powered engine existed or could be developed in time to be of use in the Second World War. A later report on the subject by S. E. Blackstone showed that the technical objections carried very little weight.

> The argument against the Meteor engine on the grounds that it is unnecessary to fit an aircraft engine into a tank is obviously not valid, even in the case of the Meteor I. The omission of the entire supercharger and wheelcase units, reduction gears, boost controls, etc. and fuel pump, oil relief valve, sump, generator drive, carburettors, induction manifolds and auxiliary drives from the camshaft, eliminate most of the features

peculiar to an aircraft engine and reduce the machining time to 40 per cent of the hours for the Merlin engine.

3. The following were the results of the cooling tests on the Meteor:

   1. The Meteor running at full throttle was better cooled than the Liberty at speeds below 19 m.p.h., using the same radiator.
   2. Using the same radiators with a blow-off pressure of 5 lb. per square inch the Meteor engine in a Mk. VI did not lose coolant at an atmospheric temperature lower than 94 degrees Fahrenheit.
   3. Using the special radiators with a blow-off pressure of 20 lb. the Meteor installation in the Mk. VI hull did not lose coolant at temperatures below 125 degrees Fahrenheit.

   'Since we doubt if anybody could exist in such a temperature', Robotham remarked, 'Leylands' remark about the cooling of this engine can but seem to be utterly unfair.'

4. This somewhat conservative outlook of the Leyland Company is probably best explained in terms of the ever-recurring choice between quality and quantity. On 24 November 1940 Mr Churchill stated in a forceful minute to General Ismay that 'at this stage in tank production numbers count above everything else'. There is no doubt that this was the wisest policy at the time and Liberty production gave numbers if nothing else. But by June 1941 the Prime Minister had changed his mind. 'It seems to me', he wrote, in a memorandum to Lord Beaverbrook, 'that the question of a much heavier tank has now come sharply to the front. The whole position must be reviewed and we must know where we are – and that soon.' Policy is changed more easily than the consequences which stem from it.

5. The cooling problem was solved by a fundamental development of fan design. Fan efficiency was raised from below 20 per cent to 57 per cent. Continued development raised it to 63 per cent.

6. The decision not to switch to the Meteor X was taken largely as a result of a survey carried out by Blackstone who pointed out that several relevant factors had been overlooked.

   The proposed change from aluminium to cast iron is not one which in itself would render the engine more suitable to production in factories now making tank engines. In fact a considerable increase in machining time is to be expected on account of the lower feeds and speeds used for machining cast-iron. it is not considered that the proposed changes will do more than offset this increase in production time'.

   Blackstone had also been asked to look at the Rover factory (which was eventually brought into the scheme) which was about to be released from the production of Armstrong-Siddeley radial aero-engines. An order for 1000 sets of Meteor components of various types was placed with the Rover Company on 27 April in response to an offer made by this company a few days earlier.

7. This point was brought home to Rolls-Royce in particular by the close contact which the chairman, Lord Herbert Scott, managed to maintain (probably against all the 'rules') with an officer who was actively engaged

in the fighting in Libya. These letters contained some particularly blunt criticism of the products of British industry. On 19 May 1942 this officer complained in one letter that 'both German and American Tanks are far superior to ours. In fact ours are disgracefully unreliable.' The letter also complained of bad workmanship inferior components and an 'almost total lack of spare parts'.

Lord Herbert Scott apparently endeavoured to explain this state of affairs in his reply, but his correspondent was not in the least satisfied. 'I am afraid', he replied on 21 August, 'that I must stick to my statement that they are badly assembled, so badly in fact that on arrival in this country all have to go into workshops and be practically taken to pieces and reassembled. . . . Luckily we are not dependent on British machines.'

8. C.f. Robotham's recommendation.

9. By the end of February 1944, 1490 engines had been delivered. In the October 1942 programme (which was itself a reduction of a previous programme), it was expected that the first 3000 engines would have been delivered by May 1944. The first 3000 engines were in fact completed by 12 October 1944. The April 1943 programme expected 4900 engines to have been delivered by this date.

CHAPTER 8

1. In many cases Rolls-Royce was itself responsible for installing the Merlin in an existing or new type of aircraft and demonstrating the improvement in performance which was obtained thereby. The outstanding example of this was the installation of the Merlin 61 in the North American Mustang fighter which, when engined by the Merlin, turned out to be one of the most outstanding aircraft of the war.

CHAPTER 9

1. For a comprehensive and detailed technical history of the Rolls-Royce gas turbines see Schlaifer, op. cit., ch. XIII.

CHAPTER 10

1. The Companion of Honour and Barony later conferred on Hives shortly after he became chairman of the company reflected the validity of Freeman's judgement and were undoubtedly accepted by Hives himself as a tribute to the great war-winning organisation which he had built up. Although a definitive biography of this remarkable man remains to be written, there is no doubt that his contribution to the evolution of Rolls-Royce ranks equally with that of Rolls, Royce and Johnson.

2. The company's auditors pointed out that if two separate companies were formed (as distinct from two separate divisions under the control of one

company), the losses of the one could not be off-set against the profits of the other for taxation purposes. The separation finally took place in 1971.

3. This committee consisted of Dr Llewelyn Smith, Mr W. A. Robotham, Mr Bleaney, Mr S. Gill and Mr D. Pearson (Later Sir Denning Pearson, chairman of the company at the time of the 1971 crisis).

CHAPTER 11

1. Most of this final chapter is drawn unamended from an article published in the December 1949 issue of the *South African Journal of Economics*. This was, at that date, the only serious study of the company's history to have been published, though there had been many books on Rolls-Royce cars and engines. To my knowledge no other study of the history of policy in the company has been published since then. It is my belief that the conclusions which I drew do not seem to have been invalidated to any significant degree by British industrial experience since 1949.

2. Rolls-Royce itself is now a nationalised concern. It is too early to say whether the judgement which I made in 1949 will be invalidated by a subsequent nationalisation of the whole industry.

3. I do not believe that the RB211 situation, although the techniques of management and estimating had developed enormously by 1970, necessarily invalidate this analysis. After all the homework had been done the decision was taken on the grounds that the firm's survival depended on it being able to stay in the market for jet engines of this type.

Index